POSITIVE DISCIPLINE

New Approach to Discipline, Positive
Parenting, and Everyday Solutions to
Parenting Problems

BY

ROBIN MURPHY

professional before attempting any techniques outlined in this book.

By reading this document, the reader agrees that under no circumstances is the author responsible for any losses, direct or indirect, which are incurred as a result of the use of information contained within this document, including, but not limited to, — errors, omissions, or inaccuracies.

Table of Contents

Introduction

Parenting is a Herculean task where joy, delight, and rewards manifest as you go on a lifetime journey with your precious child. It entails unconditional love, time, effort, and patience to ensure his proper growth and development from infancy to adulthood. When you find the perfect balance, it brings marvelous feelings that you are enabling your child with positive and proper skills to become a productive and responsible adult of tomorrow.

One of the toughest challenges that parents face is disciplining children. It is not easy, but it is a vital tool to empower your child with the necessary skills and appropriate behaviors that will help him go through life with confidence and live a happy, successful, and meaningful life in the future.

Finding the best disciplinary approach is very important because it will make or break your attempt to discipline your child. Physical punishment as a form of discipline is now becoming a taboo due to its adverse impact on the emotional and behavioral health of children. Parents are turning into a gentler, yet effective strategies like Positive Discipline.

Positive Discipline is a fantastic tool for Positive Parenting. This type of discipline is often called loving guidance because it is both kind and firm, an ideal combination that makes parents tough and supportive at the same time. Children do not live in fear when they commit mistakes or do not meet the parents' expectations. They become accountable for their actions and behaviors. It promotes and sustains a healthy, strong, and respectful parent-child relationship.

This book Positive Discipline: New Approach to Discipline, Positive Parenting, and Everyday Solutions to Parenting Problems is for all parents who aim to raise happy, positive, and well-mannered children. Struggles are real in parenting and modifying undesirable behaviors is challenging, but everything is resolved one step, one day, and one skill to teach at a time.

Make parenting an incredible, joyful journey that defines your role as a positive and loving Mom or Dad by arming yourself with the right strategies, open-mindedness, and understanding heart. Everything else follows.

CHAPTER 1

How to Correctly Discipline a Child?

Parenting is a broad term that involves adopting unique and diverse methods, techniques, and skills to raise a child successfully. It is a tough job that begins immediately when the child is born until he is ready to stand on his own feet. The enormous responsibility to mold a tiny infant into a healthy and well-rounded individual lies in your hand.

As the child grows older, the responsibility becomes more prominent and more challenging, especially when it is time to exercise your duty to discipline him. As this period commences, you face the pressure to build an open, healthy, and quality relationship with your child, while being firm about the rules and expectations that you set. It is crucial to approach parenting with laser focus like you do when completing a job or working to achieve success if you want to ensure that your child grows well-mannered, disciplined, and responsible.

The Goals of Parenting

Not all people are bestowed with a privilege to become parents, robbing them of the incredible opportunity associated with child-raising. When it happens, this life-changing event motivates you to become a better version of yourself- more loving, more patient, more responsible, more generous, and a lot more, all for the sake of your child.

There are three fundamental goals that all parents across the world share.

1. Ensuring the child's health and safety.

2. Preparing the child to become a productive adult.

3. Transmitting cultural values.

The desire to provide and protect their children at all times is inherent to all parents. It is essential, especially when your child is still an infant. Children need caring in a way that ensures their survival and protect them against harm. Parents must give children the best possible start in life- the best care, education, and food.

As a parent, you act on his behalf, shielding your child against all kinds of threats. Rushing to comfort your child at the first sign of disappointment or stopping him from trying new things because you are afraid that he might get hurt can cause more harm than good. Some parents attempt to push their children toward particular paths, but allowing them to find their own life goals is the essence of effective parenting.

There will come a time that you need to start allowing the child begins his journey, and you as a figure of authority, to begin teaching him the value of discipline. The earlier you establish certain limits for your child, the higher the percentage that he will grow into a responsible adult.

One of the challenges that parents face is how to raise a well-disciplined child without hindering his happy and healthy journey into adulthood. Discipline is vital to every family. Its goal is to help children learn self-control and choose acceptable behavior. However, it is necessary to remember that every child is born with a unique DNA that influences his temperament, character, and personality.

What is Discipline?

Discipline is described as a strategy to train someone to obey a code of behavior or rules. It is the process of demonstrating what kind of behavior is acceptable and what is not.

When you establish house rules like no watching television or using tablet until homework is done, no video games during school days, no hurtful teasing, or name-calling when playing with other siblings, you are training your child to develop self-control and understand your expectations. Simple house rules shape your child's behavior. You are teaching him the basic skills on how to manage his behavior. It is important to start while he is young to prepare him against the challenges and demands of the outside world, especially during learning years in school.

Take note that as your kid grows, his behavior changes as he goes through development. It may surprise you one day when he throws tantrums all of a sudden or become hard-headed. All behavioral changes are part of growing up, each age and stage give the child certain struggles that you, as a parent, need to understand. You need to guide him in processing these changes by not resorting to yelling, threatening, or imposing punishment.

Hence, the importance of choosing a disciplinary approach that focuses on finding the right balance. It must blend well with your parenting style, helping you feel in control without affecting the optimum development of your child's physical, mental, and emotional development. One of the approaches that can help you discipline your child without losing your self-control and maintain a healthy, loving, respectful relationship with him is **Positive Discipline**.

A. POSITIVE DISCIPLINE

Wikipedia describes Positive Discipline as a type of discipline model that focuses on the child's positive behavior. It is based on the concept that there are no bad children, only bad behaviors. Other related teachings include:

- Good behaviors can be taught and reinforced. Bad behaviors can be corrected and modified without hurting them physically or emotionally.

- Verbal punishment is sometimes more damaging than physical punishment, leaving children insecure, anxious, or fearful.

Positive Discipline aims to promote family togetherness, cooperation, and treating each other with respect. It is geared to encouraging parents to train their children in making good choices, solve problems, and make agreements that foster creativity and critical thinking. It does not rely on punishments or rewards. Instead, it utilizes the power of empathy, active listening, relationship building, and mutual respect to develop positive behaviors.

It is focused on:

- Non-punitive solutions

- Respectful and non-violent interactions

- Identifying the meaning behind the behavior

- Effective and clear communication

- Building self-esteem and capability

- Encouragement (instead of praise)

- Connection and Play

- Finding long-term solutions to develop self-discipline

- Mutually respectful parent and child relationship

- Teaching lifelong skills

- Increases confidence and competence to handle difficult situations

This approach is not new. It became popular in the 1920s when psychologists Dr. Alfred Adler and Dr. Rudolf Dreikurs introduced the idea of positive discipline to the audiences in the United States. Dr. Adler focused his attention on parenting education, actively teaching parents to treat their children with respect. He also argued that pampering and spoiling children could result in behavioral and social problems. Thus he advocated against them. The classroom management techniques were initially introduced during the same period in Vienna, Austria. However, it was only in the late 1930s that Dr. Dreikurs brought it to the U.S.

Their advocacy became the basis of Positive Discipline, an approach that is designed and developed by Dr. Jane Nelsen to help parents, mentors, and other authorities raise responsible, resilient, and independent children. It teaches essential life and social skills in a manner or approach that maintains mutual respect and encourages a deeper understanding of the discipline.

Techniques Used in Positive Discipline

• Technique 1: Creating Rules

Dr. Nelsen emphasizes the significance of establishing clear and reasonable rules. She recommends that as much as possible, rules are devised by children with the guidance of parents of authority figure and agreed upon by everyone. It will make them more accountable to follow the rules. If there is a need to modify the rules or introduce a new one, make sure that your child is informed about it and understand the reasons for the modification.

• Technique 2: Recognizing Needs

Another theory that governs Positive Discipline is that when the child misbehaves, he is displaying an unmet need that requires satisfaction. It is necessary to focus on recognizing and meeting the need instead of the behavior itself to deal with the misbehavior.

• Technique 3: Redirecting Negative Behavior

It is best to encourage positive behavior by redirecting the child's attention to something interesting and creative to resolve or stop the acts of misbehavior.

• Technique 4: Understanding the Meaning

Sometimes, misbehavior or acting out is the child's way to get attention from his parents or other people around him. It is essential to understand that children, like adults, do not do something without a valid reason. Once you understand the trigger that caused the behavior, remove or resolve it to prevent further emotional outbursts from your kid.

• Technique 5: Inspiring Intrinsic Motivation

Intrinsic motivation refers to the inherent desire of a person to feel good about oneself. The motivation comes from within and not from external sources, that include getting a reward or avoiding punishment.

All these techniques encourage the behaviors you want to see while discouraging the behaviors that you do not want to manifest in your child. In positive parenting, it is important to maintain a respectful, positive relationship with the child, while trying to decrease or increase the behavior. When things get frustrating and challenging along the way- keep your cool.

Easier said than done, right? But, when you focus on the long-term results, you will eventually say that all your efforts paid off. For now, it helps to focus on the principles of positive discipline, one day at a time. It will help you find solutions to behavioral problems, instead of temporarily stopping the problems.

The good news is- Positive Discipline is effective. Based on studies and surveys, children perform and behave better when they perceive both kindness and firmness from the parents. With high responsiveness to the feelings and needs, while setting realistic and high expectations, parents motivate children to work on concrete goals, become academically and socially successful, and less likely to engage in risky behaviors.

B. PARENTING STATISTICS

According to the National Parent Survey of Zero to Three.Org., seventy-three (73%) of parents say that parenting becomes their biggest life challenge.

- Eighty-three percent (83%) believed that positive and effective parenting strategies could be learned.

- Sixty-nine percent (69%) of parents said that if they knew about positive discipline techniques, they would use them to become better parents.

- Fifty-four percent (54%) of parents wished that they had access to the information on how to become better fathers and mothers.

The demographics showed that parents of various circumstances and backgrounds have strikingly similar beliefs about the joys and challenges of parenting. Almost everyone claimed that they are good parents. There is also a universal, intense desire to improve their parenting techniques and skills.

- A whopping ninety-one (91%) claimed that becoming parents is their greatest joy.

- Eighty-percent percent (80%) of parents from various income and education levels, races, or ethnicities strongly agreed that they are good parents to their kids.

- Eighty-seven percent (87%) stated that they work hard to become better parents.

- Seventy percent (70%) said that their lives changed when they became parents.

On Child Discipline

One of the dilemmas that parents face is how to discipline their kids. Every couple or parent has a parenting style that includes discipline strategies, which they believe are the most effective approach. Most often, they mimic or diversify their own parents' techniques.

- *Sixty-eight percent (68%)* say that they use discipline to stop the bad behaviors of their children.

- About *fifty-seven percent (57%)* are trying to figure out the best strategy to discipline their growing kids.

- *Fifty-six percent (56%)* admit that managing their children during the acts of misbehavior is a real challenge.

In the context of terrifying kids as a form of discipline, there are many debates and controversies that revolve around it because of its adverse and abusive effects on children. It is important to pay attention to several factors such as inter-generational modeling, respect/embarrassment, and power/fear to understand why a lot of parents use this strategy.

- **Intergenerational modeling** refers to the frame of reference that new parents adapt. Typically, they copy the parenting style of their parents or other influential people around them.

- **Respect/embarrassment** pertains to the desire of the parents to be in control and be respected. Any form of disobedience is viewed as a sign of disrespect.

- **Power/fear** is about the fear of parents that the behavior of their children will endanger or harm them. To ensure that their kids blend in well without being noticed or prevent being hurt (physically or emotionally), they instill fear to terrifying them.

o *Thirty-seven percent (37%) admit that they spank their children.*

o *Thirty-two percent (32%) yell to their children.*

o *Twenty-nine percent (29%) say they swat or pop their children.*

o *Twenty-eight percent (28%) hit them with an object.*

o *Twenty-three percent (23%) intentionally embarrass them.*

o *Sixteen percent (16%) force them to do a rigorous activity as a form of punishment.*

On Physical Abuse

There is a thin line that separates discipline and abuse. Every year, approximately 3 million cases of child abuse are reported. Another long-term adult study showed that 14.8% reported that they are physically abused, 12.2% are sexually abused, and 25.9% are verbally abused. Many abused children grow up with poor health and struggling against alcoholism, drug addiction, depression, mental illness, and traumas.

According to the Centers for Disease Control and Prevention, experiences of abuse and neglect during childhood result to health problems of adults. It was summarized by the World Health Organization (WHO) by stating that household dysfunction and childhood maltreatment are significant factors to the development of chronic diseases (during the later years), which are the common causes of disability and death in the United States.

One form of child maltreatment is physical abuse, which can be intentional or unintentional and can harm his health, development, survival, dignity, or self-esteem. It includes beating, hitting, shaking, kicking, suffocating, boxing ears, biting, strangling, and fatal acts like poisoning, forced ingestion, scalding, or burning.

Most physical violence against children happens inside the premise of homes, with the intent to punish them. In the U.S. alone, a large number of parents admitted that they resort to physical abuse as a form of corporal punishment to correct their kids' bad behaviors. In cases that the ordinary physical punishment becomes escalated, turning into mild to severe maltreatment or abuse, the contributory factors include parent's inability to judge their strength or control anger as well as being unaware of the vulnerability of their kids.

CHAPTER 2

How to Know If You are a Fine Parent in 2 Minutes?

What makes a fine parent? Are you doing good in your new role as a mother or a father? These simple questions may seem easy to answer, but they also provoke thinking about your parenting style and gauge how are you as a parent.

Let's say you only have 2 minutes to answer and the clock starts now!

A. Questions to ask yourself:

1. What is your concept of "discipline"?

2. Does it work?

3. Which techniques are you going to keep?

4. Which strategies are you going to let go?

5. What new tricks will you try?

How do rate yourself? Do you think or believe that you are a fine parent? There is no right or wrong answer to the given questions. Whether you give yourself a thumbs up or a thumbs down, the fact remains that you are now responsible for nurturing the growth and development of a precious child.

You don't need to be perfect to become a fine parent. Your child is not perfect, too, so don't set your expectations too high that you would neglect the most essential aspect of parenting- building and enjoying a healthy, happy, and open relationship with him.

A Fine Parent

The concept of a fine parent revolves on how you provide the essential needs for his optimum development – food, shelter, love, and discipline. If you can provide the perfect balance of all these factors, you can say that you are a fine parent. And when the child grows with adequate food for nourishment, living in a decent abode, well-loved by the family, and given a positive form of discipline, he will turn into a fine adult.

To become a fine parent, avoiding the dangers of abuse, overindulgence, or neglect is not enough. You have to focus on the following major responsibilities as delineated by The National Academy of Sciences:

1. Maintain your child's health and safety

2. Promote his emotional health and well-being

3. Prepare your child intellectually

4. Instill social skills

Various studies attested to the fact that parents who combined sensitivity and warmth, along with clear behavioral expectations, raised well-adjusted children. They practiced the Four C's of parenting:

- Care – showing affection and affection

- Consistency – maintaining a healthy, safe, and stable environment

- Choices - allowing the child to develop self-autonomy

- Consequences – applying the repercussions of choices, whether negative or positive

However, it is also true that even if the child has everything, there are circumstances that can cause problems. It happens when he is exposed to extremely difficult situations, harsh environment, peer pressure, and traumas. Any of these factors alter the character or personality of a person, whether he is a child, a teen, or a young adult.

It is also important to accept the fact that every child is unique and grows up differently from his siblings. If they grow up fine, you can proudly claim that you are a fine parent. If you have done everything for them to become independent and responsible individual, you are a fine parent. Even if at some point in your life, you and your child encounter rough moments that somehow make you question your parenting skills, they are not enough reasons to say that you are not a fine parent.

Sometimes, how your child turns out when he becomes an adult is beyond your control. Even if you supplied him with the vital four factors, genetics and environment would influence his development. Do not blame yourself. Assess the whole situation, accept what you cannot change, and continue giving him your unconditional love. It is the best quality of a fine parent.

CHAPTER 3

Discipline

Children come into being without instructions. It is up to parents to raise them properly, provide discipline, and ensure that they are well-provided. Every parent wants a well-behaved, happy, healthy, and respectful child. No one likes to raise spoiled brats, but sometimes children become too difficult to deal with, leaving parents frustrated and perplexed.

What will you do when your child becomes disrespectful and does not listen? Or deliberately defies or disobeys your request to behave.

As you encounter these problems, it is important to reinforce your role as a parent. You are the primary person who can provide a suitable discipline for your child and help him become self-reliant, self-controlled, and respectful. Other figures and authorities can help like therapists, relatives, and mentors can help, but the major responsibility rests on your shoulder.

Parenting Styles

There are three general classifications of parenting styles, according to Diana Baumbrind.

- **Authoritative.** These parents have established clear expectations and consequences. They are affectionate, flexible, and involves their children to a collaborative problem solving to behavioral challenges. The parents use rational, issue-oriented discipline to develop the children's self-control, autonomy, and other positive characteristics. They assume full responsibility for the behavior of their children. It is considered the most effective parenting style.

- **Permissive.** The parents display lots of affection to their children but only provide a little amount of discipline.

- **Authoritarian.** In between the two types are parents with clear expectations and consequences, but gives little affection to the children. They usually use forceful, absolute, and punitive discipline, expecting their kids to conform and obey. They believe that their children have no right to question their rules as long as they provide their basic needs.

These styles are modified by Dr. Jane Nelsen by categorizing them into short-term and long-term parenting.

- *Long-term parenting*

    o *Kind and Firm (uses Positive Discipline)*

- *Short-term parenting*

    o *Controlling (Punitive/Rewarding)*

    o *Neglectful (Giving up the role to be a parent)*

    o *Permissive (Overprotective/Rescuing)*

Other identified types of parenting styles:

- **Indulgent**. They are primarily concerned about the happiness of their child and do not demand much from him. In matters of discipline, they are lenient, accepting, and passive.

- **Indifferent**. These parents show low levels of demandingness and responsiveness. They just do whatever is necessary when there is a need. They rarely ask their children or assign chores to them, believing that it is important to let them live his own life.

- **Connected.** The most recent style of parenting style is associated with connectedness. They use emphatic approach to improve their connection with the child. They use Jennifer Kolari's CALM technique - Connect, Affect, Listen, and Mirror.

A. Why do you need to discipline your child?

When you hear the word discipline, what is the first thing that comes to your mind? Depending on how your parents raised you, your concept of discipline may be positive or negative. Discipline, per se, is not negative. It is a method or a set of rules that aims to prevent future behavioral issues. In short, the goal of discipline is to teach. You will be teaching your child about the principles, expectations, and guidelines set by the community or society. Some rules are written into laws, while others are unwritten, but need to be followed to avoid negative circumstances that may cause harm.

Children are typically given regular discipline to keep them safe and learn the right from the wrong. It may involve rewards and punishment to teach self-control, decrease undesirable behaviors, or develop desirable behaviors. The primary goal of discipline is to develop long-term habits that will help the child to process, manage, resolve, and live life to the fullest. And as parents, you need to be a living example of a disciplined, responsible adult.

Some of the key benefits of discipline are:

1. Helps children manage anxiety.

Young as they are, children experience anxiety due to pressure, expectations, and demands of parents, teachers, peers, and other people around them. When anxiety becomes chronic, it affects their health and well-being.

The first tendency of parents with anxious children is to shield them against the triggers and prevent negative circumstances. However, child psychologists say it is not the best way to help your kid. Remember that when your child is anxious, he needs two things- comfort and certainty. The absence of leadership and lack of guidance will make him feel lost and alone in the middle of his battle. Just like an adult, an anxious child is coping with his thoughts and emotions while going through external triggers. And when his parents expect him to make smart adult decisions, the anxiety is escalated.

What to do?

- Teach your child to face his anxiety. Eliminating the cause of anxiety may be the first thing that you want to do, but it is more important to help him cope up against the stressor. The goal is to help him process, understand, tolerate, or resolve the situation that is causing him stress. By teaching him the proper way to deal with his anxiety or overcome it, you are helping him become emotionally stronger, more resilient, and smarter.

So, the next time your child faces an uncomfortable situation that upsets him, do not immediately whisk him out or remove the thing that makes him emotional, help him handle the situation. It will cut the pattern of avoiding things as a coping mechanism. Refrain from denying your child of the opportunity to brave himself against it which in the end boosts his self-confidence.

- **Show realistic and positive expectations**. Boost the confidence of your child by teaching him that when he faces his fears and do his best, he is going to be okay. Avoid promising him that he won't fall when he is learning how to ride a bike or won't fail a test. Tell him that it's fine to fail sometimes, what matters most is that he enjoys the experience and then practice or study more to get his goals.

- **Do not belittle or amplify your child's feelings**. For instance, he is always afraid to go to the dentist. Listen to his reasons, but do not validate them by agreeing, instead explain the benefits of regular visits to the doctor. Respect his fears. Listen and read between the lines. Then, help him overcome his anxiety and encourage him to face his fears. All these acts convey the message *that "It's okay, I know you are scared, but I am here with you as you go through it."*

- **Avoid triggering and reinforcing your child's anxiety**. Avoid asking leading questions that will feed his fears like- *"Are you worried about the test?"* The better way is to ask open-ended questions like, *"How are you feeling about your test next week?"*

It is also vital not to reinforce his anxiety by saying something that seems to validate his fear. For example, he developed fear in dogs due to a negative encounter in the past and you, yourself is anxious about it and say *"It is something you should be afraid of."* However, this can be tricky because your child can pick up the underlying message that he should be worried about it because of your body language or tone of voice.

- **Cut down the anticipatory period**. The hardest period is when you are anticipating for something to happen. Spare your child from stressing him about something until you need to. Instead of discussing his dental appointment an hour before you go out of the house, try to keep the anticipatory period to a minimum to reduce his nervousness.

- **Get through it together**. Encourage your child to talk about his fears and worries. It is good to talk through and think things with your child, so you can help him handle the situation when it comes. A plan lessens the uncertainty, which is an effective and healthy way to conquer his anxiety.

- **Encourage your kid to tolerate his anxiety**. Do not stress him by setting an extremely high standard. Allow him to engage in life and learn how to tolerate anxiety by doing what he needs to do or what he wants for himself. Stressors have a natural habituation curve that eventually drops overtime as he goes through with the situation and wins over it.

- **Be a good role model**. Kids are naturally perceptive and tend to mimic their parents. Show your child how you manage anxiety and stress by being calm, tolerating it, and feeling good while going through it.

2. Teach children to make good choices.

If you want to raise a confident, independent, and resourceful child, you need to provide a healthy and positive discipline that trains him to make smart decisions. You must know the boundary of consequences and punishment. When children are disciplined and given appropriate consequences based on their age, they learn from mistakes. Moreover, punishment pushes them to find a way to escape the consequences, learning not to get caught to avoid disciplinary action.

Contrary to the old notion that discipline should be imposed when the child is old enough to understand reasons, it is important to begin early by letting him process the "normal and good behaviors." This concept becomes his internal codes (or norms), which nurtures his "conscience." Little as he is, your child's brain is capable of processing the good and the bad. He is bothered when he deviates from what you say is right and feels good when he chooses to follow you.

Furthermore, at the age of 7-10 years old, the breakthrough in terms of moral reasoning happens. The child figures out by himself what is right or wrong, not because you said it or he is afraid to be punished, but because he has internalized the values you taught, adopting them as his own and making them the primary basis to make good choices.

What to do?

- **Allow him to make mistakes**. Mistakes and failures provide tremendous lessons that are necessary for his personal growth. Do not step in unless there is potential harm. For example, your toddler is learning to walk. Allow him to navigate the short distance between you and the sofa. Do not panic when he falls on his backside and let him try again. Falling teaches him to improve his effort on his next attempts. When he grows older, teach him to manage his school allowance. If he spends all his budget during lunchtime, he will have nothing but a glass of water during afternoon recess. Watching his friends enjoying a milkshake and a cheeseburger while he has nothing to eat will teach him an invaluable lesson.

- **Do not critique your kid's attempts**. A child gains experience by making little choices. He learns how to make huge decisions by watching you do it. For instance, you are teaching him to put away his toys. He tries to stack the toys according to your instructions but fails. Do not start throwing a barrage of criticisms that lessen his initiative to do the task, making him think that he is incapable of doing it right and quit trying. Constant criticisms will make him second-guess his choice, making him afraid to make choices in the future.

Children want to feel responsible and take the initiative to learn the things that you are doing. Help your child become responsible by focusing on the result like being able to put back all the toys. Avoid sending him away and telling him that you will do it yourself or re-doing his work. Instead, show appreciation for his initiative and effort.

- **Provide options.** Empower your child by making him decide on what he believes is better such as "Do you like to take your shower now or continue playing for another 15 minutes?" or "Which one do you like the blue cup or the red cup?" These simple choices show him that you believe in his ability to make decisions and that his opinion matters.

When you offer choices, you are training him to weigh the options and think about the benefit of choosing one over the other. It forces your child to think instead of following your order. Once he makes a choice, do not offer other options. Be clear when it becomes final.

- **Stop assuming his problems**. Let your child owns his problems and learns the lessons of the situation. One classic example is when your child does not want to do his homework. As a parent, it is frustrating to see him slacking off. But remember that it is not your problem, but his problem. So, instead of constantly nagging him, allow him to face the consequences of his action or in this case, inaction. Let the consequences teach him valuable lessons. Once he is ready to change his habit, be there to reinforce his self-discipline and manage time.

- **Set limits by using "thinking words."** These words refer to statements or questions that put your child into thinking and encourage him to make the right choice. Instead of forcing or threatening when he is not eating his breakfast, why not say, "Your brother and I will be playing in the garden, you can join us after you have eaten breakfast." This statement will prompt him to act and think about the outcome, which is to join the fun.

- **Lead by example**. You need to display discipline on how you manage your time, your stressors, and other everyday matters. Show good behavior, make better choices, and stick to your principles. All these will influence your child to become more self-disciplined and gain control of his own life.

3. Help children control and manage emotions.

As a parent, your discipline strategies are naturally focused on teaching your child to become responsible and accountable for his actions. You want him to internalize the concept of self-discipline and gain a sense of control. Finally, you aim to build a positive relationship with your child.

At ages 5-10, kids begin to test the limits set by parents and break the rules. It is a vulnerable stage, which entails more patience and more focus on helping children learn to manage their emotions. Their misbehaviors or mistakes during this period are part of their growth and development. They are trying to exercise and gain solid self-control. They are also learning how to empathize and understand that their actions create an impact on other people.

Your son, for instance, knows that when he pinches his little brother, he will cry and run to you. In this scenario, your reaction is very important.

What to do?

- **Enforce a time-out**. The goal of this strategy is to help the child reflect on his misbehavior and prevent him from deeper trouble. By isolating him for a while, you are letting him step away from the situation and helping him manage his strong emotions. It is most applicable to older children. Younger kids may see this as a harsh punishment which leads to humiliation and confusion.

- **Ignore mild misbehavior**. It may not sound positive, but it works well to resolve minor problems. For example, if you refuse to give in to your child's temper tantrum, he will realize that it is not a good tactic to get what he wants. Often times, kids seek attention by misbehaving, so take away the fun by teaching him a lesson that his whining or the sudden burst of temper does not affect you. It's about choosing your battles, by pretending not to see certain behaviors and making sure that the environment is safe.

- **Redirecting attention**. It works best among young children because it is easier to move them to another activity or area or offer new toys that will stop them from misbehaving. A diversion is a tool that you can use to your great advantage, helping you to distract the attention of your child away from something he is fussing about. Ask him to go out for a walk and play in the park, instead of giving in to his demand.

- **Explain the problem and its consequences**. Help him understand that his action may lead to some serious harm or negative consequences. For instance, if he attempts to bite his playmate, it explains why biting is not good. You can tell him that "biting hurts and it is not an acceptable act." Then, discuss the consequences.

- **Encourage problem-solving**. Help your child develop a strong empathy and skills to correct his mistakes. Empathy helps him realize that improper acts create a negative impact, but can be corrected. Let the child express his own solutions by asking him what he can do to correct his mistake. For example, *"Your brother is crying now because you took his toy, what will you do to make him feel better?"*

- **Use positive discipline techniques like praise**. When you praise your kid for something he has done, he learns how to tolerate frustration and strive hard to gain success. Praise him for demonstrating good behavior and self-discipline. Giving praise encourage the child to repeat his positive acts.

4. Secures safety.

The most important objective of discipline is to keep your kid safe at all times. Safety pertains to major safety issues and general health conditions. To ensure safety, you need to impose certain rules and limits.

What to do?

- **Set house rules and limits.** They remind your child of your expectations and know that certain behaviors that are off-limits. Be clear about what you expect from him and be consistent with your boundaries. As your child matures and learns self-discipline, allow some degree of flexibility, and be open for negotiation.

- **Provide clear consequences**. Gives him a heads-up, like "I'll be counting to 5, if you do not stop, you will face the consequence." Avoid punishment as a consequence. Instead, you can enforce "time-out" to take away a privilege like watching TV or his favorite toy or something that he dislikes. It is also important to tell him when he is going to earn the privilege back (about 24 hours or less), letting him absorb the lesson of his misdemeanor.

- **Expose the child to the outside world**. Sooner or later, your child will be going out alone. He needs to be taught to follow traffic rules like looking on both sides before crossing the road.

- **Encourage the development of independence**. There is a certain point in children's lives that they begin to claim autonomy. It is a natural part of human nature, which every little child goes through. Do not see it as disobedience or rebelliousness, instead encourage your child to be independent. As he grows older, let him do his homework and make his own choices.

- **Help him make healthy choices**. Discipline teaches the child not to act on impulse. It will be helpful as he grows older and needs to choose his own. So, it is important that while he is still young, you are teaching him to eat healthy foods to prevent future health problems and instill good eating practices.

- **Discuss the underlying reasons for every rule**. For example, you do not allow your child to jump on the bed. Instead of yelling "Stop jumping" when you see him, talk to him why it is not allowed. You say that it is not safe or "If you do that, you could fall, then hit your head." By explaining the reasons, he will understand the risk and the possible consequences of his action.

B. What are the effects of lack of discipline?

It is a delight to see how well-disciplined kids behave in public or achieve their goals with ease. You know that behind them are parents who are doing their best to ensure that their children will navigate through life with confidence and make excellent choices. Like basic needs, love, and health practices, discipline is important to the child's optimum development. Without it, they are not armed with the necessary tools to face the challenges of life, including building successful relationships.

1. Lack of self-control

Among children, self-control depends on their age. It develops over the years, with significant changes during the ages of 3 and 7. But obviously, toddlers do not have the same level of self-control that older children have acquired.

Children with poor self-control or regulation skills display slow academic progress, manifest aggressive behaviors, and suffer from anxiety and depression. In the long run, they become prone to obesity, drug dependency, alcoholism, and health problems. At worst, they are susceptible to commit crimes or suicide.

2. Lack of respect towards other people

Respect is about acting in a kind, humble way during interactions with others. It includes proper greetings, manners, and conversation techniques. When kids do not show respect towards parents, playmates, and other adults, it could be embarrassing and hurtful. Disrespect is an issue that needs a positive approach. It requires a sound correction plan with the help of positive discipline, and it is crucial to correct the problem immediately.

3. Lack of appropriate behavior

Children do not know how to handle situations and tend to misbehave to hide their inadequacy. It may lead to other inappropriate acts like stealing or cheating.

4. A willful and selfish attitude

They do not like to share things and insensitive to others' feelings. Self-centered children are also stubborn and do not want to follow the rules.

5. Lack of essential social skills

Children show withdrawn behaviors like shyness, social isolation, truancy, phobia, hand flapping, staring, and anxiety. They are equipped with essential social skills like patience, empathy, and the ability to share.

6. A tendency to engage in negative behavior

They display disruptive acts like tantrums, screaming, swearing, being out-of-seat, or refusing to follow instructions. Some children show violent behaviors like head-banging, kicking, punching, running away, and biting.

7. Unhappiness

Discipline teaches children to learn how to navigate life with joy because they learn how to make good choices and develop healthy relationships among other children and adults. Without it, they lack the vital tools to process and overcome challenges, leaving them resentful, angry, and unhappy.

CHAPTER 4

Positive Approach

Parents are the biggest influences in the life of their children's development, growth, success, and happiness. As they grow older, more people come into their sphere of existence, casting various types of influence.

Parenting becomes more challenging nowadays because of the advent of modern technology, which provides easy ways to share the child's accomplishments and milestones on social media. Somehow, it makes parenting a competitive sport. But, regardless of your parenting style and strategies, the fact remains that it is your job to prepare your child for his life journey and provide him with the essential needs-structure, support, safety, and love.

Why the Positive Approach?

In contrast to the negative disciplinary approach that involves punishment in different forms, positive discipline encourages positive behaviors and decision-making. It is based on the concept that you can teach and reinforce good behavior without hurting your child physically or verbally. It teaches parents and mentors to be firm and kind at the same time. In short, positive discipline is neither permissive nor punitive.

In this approach, you are not ignoring the issues about your child's behavior. You are actively helping him handle the situations in the best way possible, without losing your temper. You remain friendly, respectful, and calm as you teach him to become more responsible and accountable for his behavior.

The positive approach allows you to use different reinforcement and consequence options after establishing rules and reasonable limits. This encourages your child to stay within limits and be responsible. In case he goes beyond the limit or defies the rules, he knows that he needs to remedy the situation to avoid the consequences.

Moreover, positive discipline allows you to teach your child to practice acceptable behaviors in a kind, yet firm approach. This method helps you communicate clearly with him what behaviors are appropriate and what are inappropriate. It does not use advocate spanking, yelling, or severe punishment, it focuses on problem-solving and encouragement.

Why teaching Positive Discipline is vital?

- It teaches a strong sense of responsibility, problem-solving skills, self-discipline, and cooperation.

- It helps children manage their emotions.

- It builds and strengthens self-esteem.

- It fosters mutual respect and trust.

- It invites children to develop their brand of significance, letting them contribute in ways that bring meaning and fulfillment.

- It forms new connections in your child's brain, which promotes better relationships.

- It guides children to handle stress in a positive and healthy way.

- It provides a more in-depth understanding that there are certain people that influence or has power to what happens in their life.

To further understand this method of discipline, you need to explore its salient points. Dr. Jane Nelsen set 5 principles to govern it.

A. Criteria for Positive Discipline

1. **It is both firm and kind.** It promotes mutual encouragement and respect that strengthens the parent-child relationship during the teaching process. Children learn good habits by imitating their parents and other role models around them. Teaching, by example, is the best way to instill discipline.

- Be respectful and kind, even if you are upset.

- Refrain from yelling, humiliating, or calling him names to prevent him from copying you when he becomes upset over something in the future. Seeing you calm and composed while dealing with the situation teaches him that this strategy is better compared to panicking or getting mad.

Aside from that, kindness encourages your child to become more receptive to reasoning, calm down, and cooperate. However, it is important to remember that kindness in this context is not synonymous with giving in or permissiveness. You are still teaching him self-discipline, in a kind way and firm way. You say NO but in a tone that is not mean or harsh.

Furthermore, you expect him to follow the limits you set and enforce consequences when he acts otherwise. This method helps your child practice cognitive thinking, helping him master skills that he will need to make more complex decision-making in the future.

2. It promotes a sense of belonging and significance. Positive discipline promotes a sense of connection, eliminating deep-seated fear of being punished or grounded. It can be demonstrated by communicating your discipline plan or rules, then explaining the consequences that you will enforce if when he disobeys or misbehaves.

If you are introducing a new rule or discipline technique, discuss it to your child so he will know how to adjust. It should not come out of the blue. In this way, you are showing him that you are working together during the learning process. It will make him feel significant and more compliant to conform to the new rule, limit, or consequence.

It works well with older children who already understand the science and reasoning behind the discipline. Kids below the age of three find it quite difficult to understand the consequences or make a sound judgment because the prefrontal cortex of the brain is not yet developed. For this age group, redirection strategies should be used. Parents should understand age-related behaviors and enforce appropriate discipline techniques.

3. **It teaches essential life and social skills**. Positive discipline is geared toward the development of skills, problem-solving, cooperation, respect, and concern for others. All these factors are important factors for the child's development and ability to contribute to the larger community, school, and home.

4. **It leads to the discovery of personal power**. This kind of discipline invites children to discover that they are capable of doing great things. They learn it when they obey and do positive deeds, or when they receive an appreciation, praise, acceptance, or a reward.

5. **Its effectiveness is long-term**. Positive discipline prepares your child to adulthood. What he is learning now will effectively help him thrive and survive in the future.

B. The Core of Positive Discipline

To fully comprehend the rationale of Positive Discipline, it is important to understand its context as an approach to instill child discipline. It originates from "disciplina," the Latin word which means teaching and comes from another term "discipulus" or pupil. It is about teaching and providing vital learning that the pupil can use in his lifetime. But over the years, discipline becomes synonymous with punishing and not teaching.

Thanks to Dr. Alfred Adler and Dr. Rudolf Dreikurs, who advocated that children be treated with respect by adults. Their ideas were later picked up by child psychologists, advocates, and authors who want to spread awareness that punishment is not the best method to fix the behavior of children or resolve problems. One of them is Dr. Jane Nelsen. She conceptualized Positive Discipline based on the teachings of these brilliant men. In 1981, she wrote and self-published the Positive Discipline book, which was picked up by Ballantine Books (now a Random House subsidiary) and published the succeeding editions including the books which she co-authored.

1. There is no such thing as bad kids, only bad behavior.

At the core of Positive Discipline is the general statement that "there is no such thing as bad children, only bad behavior." It is important for parents to bear in mind that kids are naturally good and they have episodes of acting up due to certain reasons that they cannot voice out, especially when they are young and do not know how to process their emotions.

There are two factors behind the challenging behavior of your child- the sense of not belonging (connection) and the sense of significance (contribution). When one or both of these basic needs are not satisfied, the children find a way to fulfill it, even if it requires negative action. Dr. Dreikurs aptly put it by stating that "A misbehaving child is a discouraged child."

Calling the child as "bad" for doing something negative is not healthy for his self-esteem. It usually starts when your kid continually misbehaves or throw tantrums, and you are exasperated. While trying to calm him, you slip and label him as a "bad boy" unintentionally. You can forgive yourself after that slip and quote the famous cliché that you are just human and commit mistakes, but if you keep repeating it every time he does something wrong, it will be engraved in his mind and damage his self-worth.

Positive Discipline aims to help parents learn to objectify the behavior and cut the "bad cycle." For example, instead of telling your child when he hits his younger sibling that "that's bad" or "you're such a bad boy", you may say "it is not okay to hit your brother when you are angry because he does not share his toy" and then let him understand the harm that might happen to his brother. When you objectify his behavior, you are teaching him the cause and effect. By directly addressing the "bad behavior" without using the term "bad," you are encouraging your child to make better choices and avoid hurting other people.

2. Show the child how to resolve the problem, instead of pointing out that what he did is wrong.

Redirecting the behavior of your child requires more than saying "Don't do that" or "No." It needs skills to teach him right from wrong using calm actions and words. For instance, you catch your child before he can hit his little brother, instead of saying "No hitting" or "Don't hit," tell him to "Ask his brother nicely if he wants to borrow a toy." By giving him an alternative way to get the toy, you are showing him that asking is more effective than hitting.

If he already hit his brother, it is a must to be creative with your response. One good way is enforcing a non-punitive time-out, which technically is about removing the child from the stimulus that triggers his behavior and allows him to calm down. You can cuddle him when he is very upset, let him play in his room, or ask him to sit with you and read a book. After his emotion subsides, start explaining (not lecturing) why his behavior is inappropriate. Encourage your child to give other positive options that he believes will give him the result he wants, without hurting anyone.

To change his behavior, use discipline as a teaching tool. Rather than telling him not to hit his little brother, show him the correct and acceptable behavior that will resolve the conflict and prevent him from repeating the mistake.

3. Be kind, yet firm when enforcing discipline. Show respect and empathy.

A child may insist that what he did was right, hence the importance to enforce safety rules and consequences to prevent similar incidents in the future. Listen to his story as to why he did it and win half the battle by displaying empathy, but still impose the consequence of his action to make him learn from his mistakes. Empathy makes your child feel understood, lessening his resistance, and heightened emotions.

However, even when you are disciplining your child, be respectful and when you overreact, apologize. It will teach him to respect you more and the people around him. You should behave the way you want your child to behave while showing your parental authority.

Look for the "why" behind this behavior, especially when you observe that there is a pattern. Sometimes, hitting a sibling is a silent message that he is jealous of the attention you are giving to the younger child. Whatever the cause, resolve the issue early to make your child feels secure and loved. Treat the root cause and not the symptoms.

4. Offer choices, whenever possible.

Giving your child positive choices works like magic when disciplining him. An example is when you are trying to make him sleep, and he still wants to watch TV, instead of getting angry, provide choices. "Do you like to go to bed now or in ten minutes? Ten minutes? Okay, ten minutes and then off to bed."

This approach is a win-win solution because he gets to pick the option that is okay with him and you are offering choices that are advantageous to you. By not forcing him to do something and letting him choose, you prevent power struggle. You allow him to take charge and show autonomy, within your parameters. To successfully use this technique, provide palatably, but limited choices. Eliminate options that are not acceptable to you and honor what he selects.

5. Use mistakes as learning opportunities for your child.

Use every misbehaving episode as a chance to learn invaluable life lessons. Often, the child misbehaves to achieve what he wants or when he is bored. For instance, he throws and breaks toys when he does not like them anymore. Instead of scolding him, use the opportunity to teach him the idea of giving them to his friends or donating them. If he is bored, provide other interesting activities. This will teach him the concept of displacement or finding ways to be productive and prevent destroying his properties. By empowering him with alternatives, he will be adept in making wise choices, even if you are not with him.

Use mistakes to teach your child about right and wrong. He needs to know why he is wrong, or he will continue using the act to get what he wants from you or the people around him. Just be careful not to give long lectures that will make him feel bored. Use past examples of misbehavior to strengthen your points.

6. Prevent the repeat of misbehavior by changing the scene.

The famous adage still works — "Prevention is better than cure" in the context of positive discipline. If you notice that your child keeps repeating an act, find ways to prevent it from recurring or resolve the problem.

One significant reason that you need to look into consideration is a transition. Most children do not like sudden changes, even in the ordinary routine. For instance, your child hates brushing his teeth in the morning and would do anything not to do it. Naturally, you will be frustrated because of the daily ordeal of resistance which he shows by crying, whining, screaming, hitting, or kicking.

One parent accidentally found a solution to this problem, when instead of waking the child up to eat breakfast and brush his teeth, the father took him in the backyard to let him see the squirrels and birds. The child instantly snapped out from sleepiness and enjoyed the experience. After that, when it was time to brush his teeth, the child was very cooperative.

What happens? It shows that he is not resisting the act of brushing teeth; he is against the transition from sleep to a busy day because it overwhelms him. So, the next time your child repeats his tantrums over something, get to the main cause and allows a transition time. For example, instead of rushing him to get dressed, set a timer that lets him do what he wants including getting ready. Ask him- ¨Do you need 20 or 30 minutes to get ready?¨ By letting him decide, he becomes in-charge of the allotted time but knows that he needs to show up dressed up before the time is up.

7. Be clear and consistent with your expectations and boundaries.

Children always find ways to push beyond the limits or find loopholes to satisfy their whims. He will attempt to test the limits to see your reaction or challenge you to know what will happen. So, it is necessary to talk to your child about the boundaries you set and what you expect from him. Explain the corresponding consequences when he violates limits or house rules.

Some of the simple rules include no-name calling, no TV until the homework is done, or no hitting allowed. You may also place a warning system like one warning means loss of one privilege like using the tablet to play games, two warnings entail not using it for one day, and so on. Be creative when setting consequences. Make sure that you are not depriving him of basic needs and he is safe.

It is also essential to be consistent and follow through (do what you say) because it shows that you are serious about discipline. By being consistent, you are teaching him self-discipline, self-control, and other valuable lessons in life that will come in handy when he becomes an adult. Discipline requires a consistent application to be effective. Over time, he will recognize that his behavior and actions lead to consequences that he abhors.

8. Use questions, state facts, or single-word reminders, instead of demanding or ordering him to comply.

When your baby grows into a toddler, you need to find language that will make him comply and cooperate. Using respectful words is essential to make him obey you without saying the words "Stop" and "No." Connecting with your little child required breaking down communication barriers since he is still developing his speech skill.

It is much better to say "Please look to your left and right before crossing the street," instead of ordering "Don't cross the street without looking on your right and left." The word "don't" serves as the modifier that confuses a little child. Say for example, even if you cry out "Don't jump in the puddle," your 2-year old kid still jump in and wonder why you are annoyed.

Treat and talk to him like an adult. Instead of ordering him, use positive phrasing, open questions, single-word reminders, or facts.

- Use, "Shall we get up now?" instead of "Time to get up!"

- "Shall we put these away, so nobody trips over them?", instead of yelling, "Put them away!"

- "Your face is covered with chocolate! What shall we do about it?" instead of "Wipe your face."

- "Light" instead of "Turn off the light after using the toilet."

- "Kind words, please." instead of "Don't speak like that."

- "Water is wasting," instead of "You are wasting water."

- "We need to look after your little brother.", instead of "Don't hit the baby!"

- How can we solve this problem?

- What will say to your brother instead?

- You like to play with the toy, don't you? What will you say to him?

Be generous with reasons, background information, facts, and explanations, so your child will better comprehend why he is not allowed to do something or why he needs to do it.

9. Involve him in problem-solving by working together as a team to find a mutually-agreeable solution.

Children behave better on their free will when they see parents as allies. By giving your child a voice and the opportunity to be heard, he becomes more cooperative. Brainstorm solutions together and allow him to provide suggestions on matters that ensure the safety and well-being.

When you involve your kids rather than giving them the solution that you believe is right, you are showing him that you respect his opinions. It will be easier to teach him problem-solving skills and encourage to think creatively. So, whenever your child exhibits behavioral problems, call his attention and discuss what seems to be a problem. Give him a chance to share his feelings and needs, then find a solution that is acceptable to both of you. You can write down the myriad of ideas that come up but do not evaluate yet. Finally, decide together, which among the suggestions will work to resolve the problem.

10. Allow your kid to face natural consequences.

There are two types of consequences- natural and made-up. The latter are those that you make to suit your needs and propel him to comply. Some experts say that made-up consequences are punishments in disguise.

Categorically, *made-up consequences* come in forms of immediate consequences, fair consequences, and logical consequence.

- Immediate consequences help you teach the child to realize that his behavior is tied up with a consequence. An example is losing his phone privileges for a week when you find out that he is lying about getting his homework done.

- Fair consequences are those that are reasonable and not overly harsh. If you ground him or prevent him from using electronics for one month, your kid would not think it is fair, and you are doing an injustice. He will fight the consequence, every step of the way and will try to defy it when you are not around.

- Logical consequences benefit children with specific behavior problems. An example is disallowing him to play with his toys if he refuses to put them back on the shelf. By linking the consequence with the problem, you let your child see that his choice has direct consequence.

Natural consequences are part of natural growth. When you allow your kid to make mistakes and experience the natural results that arise from his misbehavior, you are showing him that inappropriate actions can lead them into trouble or face immediate consequences that are beyond your control.

For example, he touches the hot pot and gets his hand burned. The pain is the natural consequence, teaching him not to do it again. If he breaks his toy, he will have no toy to play with. Use this method when it is applicable, but remember to monitor the situation to prevent real danger. And remember to apply age-appropriate consequences.

C. Positive Parenting

Positive Parenting is defined as a style of parenting that emphasizes mutual respect. It is also referred to as gentle guidance, affectionate guidance, or loving guidance which places or keeps the child on the correct path. It uses positive discipline, instructions, and reinforcements which are geared at training the child to become a self-disciplined, responsible, and confident person. It involves teaching the child the who, where, when, what, and why of every situation. Its primary goal is to develop a deeply-committed, open, healthy, and strong relationship between the child and the parent.

This type of parenting is focused on using positive methods to raise children, resisting the temptation to utilize punitive or harsh words to discipline them. It is the best approach for parents who want to discipline their children without breaking their spirit since it essentially supports the capacity to learn with respect, trust, and love. A lot of studies have shown that this parenting style yields better results in terms of children's academic performance, mental health, emotional growth, and behavior.

It is an approach that helps children feel connected, connected, capable, and cooperative. It is not just about letting go of punishment or being permissive. Positive parenting is choosing to become actively involved in connecting and supporting their optimum growth and development. Generally speaking, positive parenting nurtures the child's self-esteem, sense of mastery, ability to interact, and belief in the future by living a productive, open, and healthy life.

Key Elements of Positive Parenting

- Imagine or understand the point of view of the child during challenging times.

- Provide consistent and age-appropriate rules, limits, and expectations.

- Respond with sensitivity and interest to the cues that the child displays.

- Recognize the child's abilities, strengths, and capabilities to learn, then celebrating them to reinforce the development.

- Enjoy moments of connection.

- Work to attain a balanced time for child needs and parental needs.

- Understand that missteps are part of rearing a child and sometimes, parenting can be stressful.

- Learn how to regulate your behaviors and emotions before responding to your child.

- Seek support, help, and parenting information if necessary.

Studies show that the experiences of the child in his first three years of life are influenced by the quality of caring that he receives from his parents. The efforts to nurture, support, and raise him set his path to success and happiness. Moreover, the zero to five years of his age are the most critical because they see, hear, and pick up what you do or say. His young brain is recording and assimilating everything, processing them as truth and proper. Your habits become his new habits.

Effects of Positive Parenting

Positive parenting encourages children to respond to gentle guidance, improving their behavior, and developing self-discipline. In the absence of threats and punishments, children discover their strengths, power, and capabilities. It teaches children to accept their flaws or weaknesses and work to improve them.

It offers a lot of benefits which include:

A. Maintaining quality parent-child relationship.

A nurturing relationship between you and your child is the foundation for the development of good character traits, behavior, and confidence. Positive parenting is characterized by firm, loving guidance that builds a stronger connection and relationship. When you consider the long-term effects of positive parenting to your child, you know that you are on the right track.

The parental relationship is the most significant and influential connection that sets the bar for the child's positive disposition in life, success, and behavior. The strong bond fosters better decision-making, boosts self-esteem, encourage autonomy, and promote cooperation.

As a parent, you need to find the right balance of enforcing discipline, while showing your unconditional support and love. Punishment can destroy your relationship with your child and can lead to misbehavior. With positive discipline, you set limits and reinforce expectation by guiding him gently yet firmly, helping him improve his behavior rather than staying angry with you.

Kids are naturally attention-seeker when they are young, so it is important to fill their "attention basket" with lots of positive and proactive attention that will teach them to be responsible, respectful, and more cooperative. When their needs are met, they will not try to push the buttons to get the attention by throwing tantrums, misbehaving, and acting out in negative ways.

- **Be involved**. Enrich your relationship by connecting with your child using an age-appropriate approach. If your child is still a toddler, play with him, work on fun and creative projects, and teach him to read. If you have an adolescent child, challenge him in his favorite video game or sport. This technique will make him see you as an approachable parent.

- **Give emphasis on family time**. Make it a rule to eat dinner together or do something together during weekends. By establishing a regular family togetherness, you are teaching your child the importance of family as a unit.

- **Set a one-on-one time for your child**. Spending quality time with your child is priceless. It helps you monitor his progress and development, making him feel your presence in every step of his journey as a person. Recognize his talents, strengths, and interests. Use the time to instill positive discipline by talking about situations that he considers difficult and find ways together to resolve the problems permanently. Build a meaningful and special bond by engaging in fun or educational activities.

- **Get in touch with his academic and extracurricular activities**. No matter how busy you are, making an effort to learn about his daily activities will make him feel loved and important. Ask about his friends at school, sit down with him when he is doing homework, help him review before the test, attend his school events, or invite his friends over.

B. Taking responsibility for actions

Become the model of accountability by being humble and honest to admit that you are wrong. Teach him the importance of saying sorry and being responsible for his action or reactions over matters that affect relationships.

Before you can effectively teach your kid about taking responsibility for his actions, it is necessary to recognize and understand the "why" that triggers his behavior. There is a reason why he misbehaves, not just to get into trouble or annoy you. As a parent, you have to find it out in ways that will not offend, hurt, or embarrass him.

- **Respond, but do not react**. Avoid overreacting and take a deep breath. Do not force him to apologize or become accountable immediately. Give time for both of you to calm down.

- **Make it safe for him to come forward**. Once everyone is calm, let him approach you and explain his behavior or admit the truth. Another option is to approach him and talk about what happened. If he admits his wrongdoing and apologizes, you need to acknowledge the effort, discuss how it can be prevented in the future, and enforce the corresponding consequence of his action.

- **Stick to your rules and limits**. No matter how pitiful his pleadings or how sweet he becomes after his misbehavior, it is important to be consistent with your discipline strategy. Don't give in if you want to convince him that you are serious about the rules.

- **Talk about action or behavior, not the person**. Instead of pointing out your child's flaw, focus your attention to his behavior, and find the reason behind. Let him voice out his sentiments, feelings, and thoughts. Empathize with his struggles, listen to what he is telling you, read between the lines, and work together to find an appropriate solution that will prevent the recurrence of the action.

C. Being respectful to others

One of the goals of positive discipline and positive parenting is fostering mutual respect. Respect is a two-way process. If you want to raise a respectful child, it is important to model the behavior. Home is the first place where he learns about this fundamental virtue, so you need to teach respect as early as possible.

- **Lead by example**. Kids are very impressionable. They naturally mimic the habits of people who are around them while growing up and looks up to them as role models. Start teaching your child the value of respect, living a respectful, and leading a caring and kind life.

- **Use respect as a tool for him to get what likes**. In the adult world, people who show respect are most likely to get what they want. Teach this to your child by only giving the something he wants when he is respectful. He will soon realize that it is a quicker and smarter way rather than throwing a fit.

- **Encourage activities that require cooperation and sharing**. One example that teaches these virtues is a board game. Every player needs to respect the time that other players take to consider their moves.

- **Be patient**. Patience is a manifestation of respect. To teach it effectively, you should not display impatience when you are dealing with him. If he observes that you are not practicing what you are telling him, he will not imbibe the true essence of patience.

D. Knowing the difference between right and wrong.

Recent studies revealed that 19-21 months old babies could understand the sense of fairness or the right from the wrong. The quality of care that children experience in the early months of his life lays the foundation of a positive parent-child relationship. The first five years of their lives are crucial periods in terms of moral, social, and emotional development. Their understanding of justice and fairness expands as they grow.

At ages 0 to 1, the infant learns right from wrong through experience. He feels that something is wrong when he is wet or hungry. If he is properly attended and nurtured, he feels good and right. By the time he is 1-year old, he can communicate his feelings through actions and preferences, initiate contact, imitate, and develop a deeper understanding of what is right to do and what is not.

At ages 1-3, the toddler learns to understand the concept of rules. He responds and stops his attempt if you tell him not to do something. However, sometimes, he cannot resist acting impulsively like grabbing a toy from another child. At this period, he still cannot truly distinguish the right and wrong acts. The child relies on you or other figures of authority to define them for him. You need to consistently teach him that "being right" means obedience and not hurting others. It is important to offer continuous guidance and teach about acceptable/unacceptable behavior and make him realize the consequences for his actions.

At ages 4-5, the preschooler child begins to develop his own ideas of what is right and wrong based on what he sees and learns from the family. As his social exposure and interactions increase, the child's moral intelligence grows too. He becomes more aware of acceptable behavior and begins to develop a stronger sense of justice. At this stage, you need to be more vigilant and consistent with your reminders.

- Initiate discussions about ethical situations and encourage your child to talk about his feelings. It leads to the development of values and ethical behaviors that will guide him in his lifetime.

- Let him understand that people have different feelings and thoughts. This will develop his capacity to observe and respect the feelings of other people, learning to respond with concern and care.

- Help your child understand his feelings. Make him realize that feelings are not wrong or right, but the way he acts or reacts makes a big difference.

- Regularly discuss with your child your decisions or behaviors in the context of right and wrong.

E. Making good and wise decisions.

Decision making is a vital skill that your child needs to develop to become successful in all aspects of his life, especially when he becomes an adult. The choices and decisions he makes dictate the path and direction of his mature life. Thus, the importance of teaching your child how to make wise decisions.

It is necessary to teach him as early as possible because once he goes out to start interacting with the outside world, there are external influences that will attempt to steal the decision-making from him. The popular culture, for instance, will try to short-circuit his decisions by making him push the "hot buttons" that are linked to peer acceptance, stimulation, or physical attractiveness. Most children who are good in decision making become victims because they are easily swayed by the popular culture.

Raise smart kids who are adept in decision-making by:

- Encouraging him to decide by himself. This will help him to become independent and competent to stand on his own. If he makes a bad decision and suffers from the consequences, let him learn from the experience so he will be more careful in the future.

- Giving him small doses of choices, so he will not be overwhelmed. One example is letting him pick between two shirts- *"Which do you want to wear today- the blue shirt or the white shirt?"* As he grows older, expand the choices and make him see whether his decision is bad or good. Your child will soon realize that whenever he makes sound and right decisions, he gains a great amount of fulfillment and satisfaction.

- Teaching him to stop before leaping or thinking before making a choice. Train your child to ask himself several questions before deciding on the matter at hand. *"Is it essential to my life or growth?", "Do I need it or just want it?", "Do I have other options?", "What are the consequences of acting on it?"*, and the most important *"Is this decision in my best interest?"*. If he learns to imbibe these pertinent questions and use them before deciding on small to big decisions, your child can withstand the pressure of his peers and popular culture.

F. Being honest, trustworthy, and loyal.

Before you can effectively discipline your child, it is important to affirm or reaffirm your connection by being honest with your feelings.

- If you want him to study, tell him how proud you are for the high score he got during the last examination.

- If you are nervous about how he runs across the parking lot without looking first on both sides, tell it to him.

When you impart your feelings, he is more likely to follow your wishes, creating a life-lasting pattern of making him anticipate or be concerned with others' feelings before acting.

Positive parenting creates trustworthy and loyal children who are motivated by excellence. They learn to achieve their goals not because they fear punishment, but because they want to feel the satisfaction of accomplishment by performing well.

Signs of trustworthiness

- Telling the truth despite the knowledge that there is a consequence of his action

- Willingness to try again after failing the first time

- Returning things that they borrow in the same condition when they receive them

- Following through their responsibilities and chores

- Keeping promises

- Not telling secrets that are shared with him

- Being loyal to friends, family, country

CHAPTER 5

A New Look on Misbehavior

Children at some point of their lives misbehave, throw uncontrollable fits, display repetitive tantrums, and act out negatively. Most parents do not understand why they changed from docile and well-behaved kids into defiant ones?

Is misbehavior age-related? Is it a normal phase of growing up? Can it be prevented before its occurrence? Before exploring the many reasons why children misbehave, you need to understand the normal phase of child development.

Accordingly, each child has six domains of development which are:

1. **Physical Development** – It refers to the development and growth of his body. It includes nutrition, fitness, dental health, and general well-being.

2. **Intellectual Development** – It refers to the growth of cognitive thoughts, thought processes, and other brain functions.

3. **Language Development** – It is associated with the development of communication skills like speech, writing, body language, and reading.

4. **Emotional/Social Development** – It is about understanding oneself and others, developing self-esteem, experiencing varied emotions, as well as establishing interpersonal relationships.

5. **Moral Development**- It is the development of empathy and the child's ability to decipher the right from the wrong.

6. **Sexual Development** – It is the awareness of the distinct differences between male and female bodies, attitudes, and emotional responses. During the latter part of growing up, there are hormonal changes that stimulate physical desire and the capability for conception and giving birth.

Each area has a normal path of development that influences the behavior, personality, and temperament of children. Every area has a beginner, intermediate, and advanced level, the reason why some children are more capable of following rules and adapting to experiences and others are not. Once you have a solid understanding of these domains and their levels, you become adept at how to raise a well-mannered child.

Another noteworthy to study is Erik Erikson's eight areas of Psychosocial Development, which are based on Sigmund Freud's theory of psychosexual development. It is focused on the resolution of issues to help children become a complete, productive, and successful person. It revolves around the mastery of attitudes, skills, and ideas at every stage.

1. **Trust vs. Mistrust (From birth-12 months old)** – At this stage, infants begin to learn that adults around them can be trusted. They develop their sense of trust when their needs are met, seeing the world as a predictable and safe place. On the other hand, if the caregivers/parents are not responsive to their needs, they see the world as unpredictable, which leads to fear, mistrust, and anxiety. If they are treated with cruelty or their needs are inappropriately met, they may grow up with a sense of distrust.

2. **Autonomy vs. Doubt/Shame (From age 1-3 years old)**. Toddlers start to explore the world, act to get results and learn to control their actions. They begin to show preferences on what kind of toys, foods, or clothing they like. At this age, toddlers' main agenda

is to address the issue of autonomy versus shame/doubt by establishing independence. It is the "ME DO IT" growing phase. Parents should remember that any denial of the child's input for basic decisions like choosing his clothes will impact his sense of autonomy and make him doubt his ability to choose properly and that could lead to feelings of shame and low self-esteem.

3. **Initiative vs. Guilt (From 3-6 years old)**. During this preschool years, children become capable of asserting control and initiating activities through play and social interactions. The main task of the kids during this stage is to master the skills in achieving goals while getting along with others. When parents allow children to explore within certain boundaries and support their choices, they develop a sense of purpose and become more confident. Kids who are not successful during this stage because of over-controlling parents or bad choices may develop guilt feelings and experience deep-seated shame.

4. **Industry vs. Inferiority (From 6-12 years old)**. This is the elementary school age and the stage where children begin to face the dilemma of establishing a solid identity by exploring different roles and

discovering their "adult" selves. It is an extremely critical period because it sets the path to the future. Teens who successfully adopt a positive role can remain true to their values and beliefs when facing other people's intervention, while those who struggle to establish a strong sense of identity may face a continuous struggle to "find" themselves as they go through life.

5. **Identity vs. Role Confusion (From 12-18 years old).** This is the adolescence stage where children begin to face the dilemma of establishing a solid identity by exploring different roles and discovering their "adult" selves. It is an extremely critical period because it sets the path to the future. Teens who successfully adopt a positive role can remain true to their values and beliefs when facing other people's intervention, while those who struggle to establish a strong sense of identity may face a continuous struggle to "find" themselves as they go through life.

6. **Intimacy vs. Isolation. (From 20-early 40s)**. At this stage of early adulthood, people become concerned about personal relationships. They prepare themselves for the prospects of sharing life with

others. Adults with positive self-concept are more likely to build successful intimate relationships, while those with a weak self-concept usually experience emotional isolation and loneliness.

You may or not be around during these last stages of your child's life, but what you teach him during childhood continues to guide him through the negative issues that come up.

- **Generativity vs. Stagnation (From 40-mid 60s)**. It is middle adulthood, where people engage in productive and meaningful work to contribute to the development of others and society. This period is where adults start contributing to the next generation by giving birth (females) or caring for others. Those who fail to master the task may experience stagnation, isolation, and a sense of failure for not leaving a significant legacy in the world. Moreover, they will be disinterested in pursuing self-improvement and productivity.

- **Integrity vs. Despair (From the mid-60s to the end of life)**. It is called late adulthood, where people begin to reflect on their journey in life- either feeling a sense of satisfaction or failure. Those who are proud and satisfied with their achievements feel a strong sense of integrity and look back with few regrets. But those who are not successful in their attempts feel that their lives are wasted and look back with lots of "should have," "could have," and "would have," waiting the finality of life with feelings of despair, depression, and bitterness.

Understanding these domains and psychosocial development stages are the key tools that parents can use to help their children grow with confidence and armed with skills to gain positive outcomes from infancy to late adulthood.

Now, it's time to unlock the coded messages of misbehavior.

Why Children Misbehave?

Most often than not, children who display misbehavior are discouraged kids yearning for *significance and a sense of belonging.* Social psychologist Dr. Alfred Adler affirmed in his researches that humans are naturally "hard-wired" towards these two concepts that they believe define who they are.

Positive parenting guides parents to become proactive and ready to ward off future misbehavior by meeting the emotional needs of their children. Imagine your child having two buckets- the first one is labeled Belonging and the other one is labeled Significance.

- **Belonging**

It basically refers to a connection or how the child fits into a group (family, classroom, friends, or community). If the connection is lost, altered, or absent, this results in insecurity and other negative feelings.

You can fill up this bucket with an assurance that he plays a very important role in the family and he is loved. Spending regular time with him every day is another excellent way to fill his bucket.

- **Significance**

It is a feeling that comes from knowing that one has contributed to the whole in a meaningful way. People feel significant when they believe that they make a difference in the group, community, or society by contributing something meaningful. Young as they are, children are also eager to contribute, cooperate, and help to solve problems through various opportunities at home or school.

You can fill up this bucket by empowering him to complete simple, age-appropriate tasks and letting him help you around. You can involve him in making meaningful decisions and choices throughout the day, making him feel valued.

It is important to remember that young kids do not have the skills to revert to the significance and belonging after feeling discouraged. They usually feel confused and mixed up, so parents should be careful when reacting to their failed attempts.

Some scenarios that display the child's attempts to reclaim significance and belonging:

- A child who feels dethroned by the arrival of the newest member of the family will show "regression" to test and explore his new role in the family. If the parent enforces a lot of time-outs as a consequence of his misbehavior, the child will interpret it as messages that he does not fit or belong in the family and he better become more creative in his "regression" acts.

- A child who receives constant criticisms or being compared to other children and made to feel inferior will stop trying and withdraw to prevent being noticed. He feels it is safer and better to pull away since he does not belong and is not perfect.

- A child who feels hurt and lonely may attempt to hurt others, so he will not be alone in his pain and misery. If the parent, teacher, or caregiver punishes him in any form, his feeling of discouragement and pain are magnified.

- A child who engages his parents or other parental figures in constant power struggles believes that it is the only way to control or be the boss. When adults fail to recognize that the child is requesting for more power or control over his life and fall straight into his trap, the struggles begin.

Seeking significance and belonging can be tough even to adults. So, how do you expect growing children who are new to all these things to know the process to regain their place in the family or group where he is a member? Misbehavior is a form of communication where children speak to adults in coded messages when they suddenly feel the threats in their sense of belonging and significance.

It is vital to understand that all healthy and normal children misbehave because they are growing, exploring, discovering, learning, and experimenting. It is the duty of parents to guide, discipline, and make their journey in life more fun. You don't want to raise a grumpy child who will grow as a grumpy adult, right? So, brace yourself and become a more positive parent!

Reasons why kids misbehave:

Unmet Needs

The basic needs are not provided. Children need adequate sleep, rest, and food. If their basic needs are not satisfied, they become cranky, irritated, or bored.

Other needs include:

- The need for acceptance and validation of their feelings or thoughts

- The need for a safe place to explore

- The need for attention, stability, and closeness

- The need for unconditional love

- The need to be heard, respected, and understood

- The need to make their own choices and given opportunities to become independent

More Independence

At the age of two, children usually demonstrate a desire to become more independent. They start to show control over certain areas where they recognize they have the power to feel in control, which usually upsets and frustrates the parents. Examples are situations like brushing teeth, dressing, eating, and sleeping. Struggles between parents and children are real in these areas.

Attention

When parents do not notice that their kids are trying to catch their attention, they learn that the easiest and effective attention-getter is throwing a tantrum or misbehave. Some children are naturally egocentric and want the world to revolve around them. Kids who feel neglected even try to get in trouble to gain their parents' attention.

Control and Power

Refusal to follow instructions and follow the request of their parents are indications that children want to be in control, along with lashing out when reprimanded.

Revenge-Seeking

Children who lash out with hurtful statements like *"I don't love you" or "I hate you"* or breaks the toys of his younger sibling and other kids usually feel that they have little or no value.

Lack of Experience to Fully Understand Rules or Requests

They do not completely understand your request or the rules you set. One example is asking your kid to calm down. If he has no prior experience of calming down, he does not know its meaning and how to be calm, unless you already taught or showed him the method. Do not assume that he remembers everything you teach. It takes practice and time for children to master the skills to communicate and solve problems. The learning process for most children takes a lot of repetition.

Sensitivity to Strong Emotions

Children become frustrated, stressed, overwhelmed, or angry when experiencing strong emotions. Thus they misbehave to release their feelings. Changes, even the positive ones are stressful for them, so do not make simultaneous changes that will affect their sense of stability and normal routine.

Testing the Rules

Sometimes, children defy the rules to know if their parents mean what they say. If they observe inconsistency, they will try misbehaving again.

Just Curious

Children are naturally curious about everything around them. They like to try new things or experimenting. When parents do not approve of the activity they want to try. They display inappropriate behavior.

Inadequacy

In contrast, when children feel inadequate, they refuse to try new things or give up easily. If their parents push them to continue, they react by throwing fits or crying out loud.

Imitate Others

They tend to mimic the behaviors of people they see at school, at home, on social media, and TV.

To help you stop unwanted behavior of your child, always ask yourself these four helpful questions:

1. Does my child have an emotional or physical need that is not met?

2. Do I need to set aside my task for a while and address his misbehavior by connecting with him?

3. Does he need better instruction or a safer option?

4. Do I need to set a clear and kind limit for him?

How to Break the Pattern of Misbehavior?

For each behavior, there is an attached belief that triggers the action. Most parents and adults around kids only see the behavior and try to address it with available solutions that include discipline. They do not delve further to find out the underlying cause, the belief behind it, and the needs that require fulfillment.

Both Dr. Alfred Adler and Dr. Rudolf Dreikurs believed and taught that a discouraged child is a misbehaved child. It is generated by the belief that he does not belong. Of course, parents find it hard to believe and would say "How can he think about not belonging?", "Didn't he know or see how much I love him?" or "This is not making any sense at all!"

The way children think is different from adults during the early years of their existence because they still cannot completely understand and process the situations, experiences, changes, and other things that are happening in their lives. They have a unique, raw way to perceive the world and create their own beliefs. This is why getting into your child's world is necessary if you want to understand their "private logic," which is far different from your own.

Kids misbehave because they believe that it is the best way to gain a sense of belonging. This mistaken belief generates inappropriate acts that prompt the parents to react negatively, which for children is a confirmation of their belief that they are not valued (significant) or do not belong. Unless the parents learn to decode the reason for misbehavior, the pattern will continue.

There is only one way to change the behavior- by changing or correcting the belief.

Dealing with the belief does not necessarily mean that you will not be dealing with the behavior. You will be hitting two birds with one stone. One of the concepts that govern Positive Discipline is to identify the belief behind every behavior. This type of discipline empowers the Positive Parenting approach by helping parents recognize the reasons why their kids act as they do then work to alter their beliefs, instead of just attempting to change the behavior. Resolving the issue becomes more effective because you are aware of the belief and the behavior that it triggers.

Steps to break the misbehavior using the Mistaken Goal Chart:

1. Identify the challenging behavior of your child.

2. Describe your feelings about the behavior in one word. Be specific and do not use ¨frustrated¨ because it is a broad and generic feeling.

3. What is your usual reaction whenever your child manifests the challenging behavior?

4. If you are your kid, what will be your response to what you say?

   o What will you feel?

   o What will you think?

   o What will you do? (The action or response is the clue that points out the belief behind the action).

1. Break the code by identifying what your kid needs. (Use the Mistaken Belief Chart)

2. Select a suggestion that you would like to apply the next time your child shows the challenging behavior. Discuss why it might help and encourage him to change his belief in finding significance and belonging.

3. Write the results. It does not instantly or totally change his behavior, but it may encourage him to make at least one new decision.

Practice until these steps until they become second nature to you.

Understanding the Mistake Belief Chart

Child's Goals	Feelings of the Parent or Teacher	Reactions	The Child Response	The Belief behind the behavior	Possible Contribution of Adults	Coded Messages	Empowering and Proactive Responses
UNDUE ATTENTION (to get special attention or keep others busy)	Annoyed Worried Guilty Irritated	Coaxing Reminding Doing the things that the kid should be doing	Stops but later resumes with the same or different act Stops the act once he receives full or one-on-one attention	"I belong only when you noticed or give me special attention" "I am only important when I keep you busy with me."	"I don' trust you to handle disappointment". "I feel guilty when you are unhappy."	NOTICE ME INVOLVE ME	Involve the child by giving a useful task Tell him what you will do (I love you and we will play later) Set up a routine Avoid special services

							Plan special time Set up nonverbal signs as communication Engage him in problem-solving Show faith for his ability to deal with feeling by refraining to rescue or fix it for him. Say it once and then act Ignore [or touching without word] Use family or class meetings
REVENGE [to get even]	Hurt Disgusted Disappointed Disbelieving	Getting even Taking the behavior Personally Retaliating Thinking "How can you do it to me?"	Gets even Escalates the behavior or use another tactic Hurt others Damage property like toys	"I feel I don't belong so I will inflict pain to others" "I cannot be loved or liked"	"I expect that you know why I give more focus on your grades in school rather than as a person" "I give you advice because I	I AM HURT VALIDATE MY FEELING	Build trust Apologize Display reflective listening Show you care Act, don't just talk Acknowledge his hurting Share your feelings Make amends

					believe I am helping "	-	Avoid punishments or retaliations Encourage strengths Avoid taking the behavior personally Put the kids in the same boat Use family or class meetings

ASSUMED INADEQUACY [to be left alone and give up]	Hopeless Helpless Despair Inadequate	Giving up Over-helping Doing for Showing lack of faith	Passive Retreats further No response No improvement Avoid trying	"I am unable and helpless." "I'll convince others not to expect a lot from me because I believe I do not belong." "I cannot do it right so why try"	"I thought doing things for you was my job." "I am expecting you to live up to my high expectations."	DON'T GIVE UP ON ME SHOW ME SMALL STEPS	Stop criticisms Break tasks to small steps Give time for training Focus on assets Make the tasks easier until such time that the child has experienced success. Set up opportunities for success. Encourage positive attempts, no matter how small they are. Build on his interests. Show faith in his abilities

							and talents Don't pity Enjoy the child Teach skills by showing him how, but refrain from doing it for him Don't give up Use family or class meetings

| MISGUIDED POWER (to be the boss) | Angry Defeated Challenged Threatened | Giving in Fighting Wanting to be right Thinking "I'll make you" or "You can't get away with it." | Defiant compliance Passive Power Intensifies the behavior Feels he has won whenever he sees his parent/teacher is upset | "I belong only when I am in control, a boss, or proving that no one else can boss me" "You cannot make me" | "You must do what because I am in control" "I believe that the best way to motivating you to achieve more or do better is to tell you what to do, lecturing, or punishing you when you fail to do it" | LET ME HELP YOU GIVE ME CHOICES | Be firm and kind Don't give in Don't fight Act, don't talk Acknowledge that you cannot redirect him to positive power or make him do something by asking for help Offer limited choices Let routines be the boss Withdraw from conflict and calm down Develop mutual respect |

							Decide what will you do Get his help to set few and reasonable limits. Practice follow-through. Use family or class meetings

It is quite tricky and difficult when you are emotionally triggered by your child's misbehavior, however, remembering that he is also being challenged by his mistaken beliefs and overwhelming emotions, putting him into a helpless situation and attempting to cope up with the limited ways he knows.

Misbehavior is a silent plea, message, or call from your child that he needs guidance from you or someone he trusts. It does not always seem what it is and does not require "discipline." It is your tool to teach, guide, and train him to overcome his struggles.

CHAPTER 6

Awareness of Logical Consequences

Teaching your child about consequences is an effective way to develop his sense of responsibility and become accountable for his actions. In effect, he chooses the consequence, he experiences. Whatever his age, it is necessary to be consistent in disciplining him, stick to the rules you set, and enforce the consequence of every misbehavior.

A. Logical Consequences vs. Natural Consequences

There are two common forms of consequences- logical and natural.

Natural consequences refer to the inevitable outcome of his action. For instance, your child does not want to wear a jacket. While on the outside, he feels cold and uncomfortable, but he has no jacket to warm himself. It is the consequence of his choice not to bring his jacket. He cannot blame others for his misery because it is his choice. The learning experience teaches him a lesson to always bring a jacket.

Logical consequences are basically the result of your child's irrational acts that may endanger his safety or life. They are formulated to keep him away from hard and require adult intervention to be enforced. When devising them, it is important that they must not affect the mutual respect between the parent and the child. Logical consequences must be problem-related and reasonable.

B. The 3 R's and H of Logical Consequences

This simple formula identifies the four major criteria that you need to observe to ensure that the logical consequences are solutions to inappropriate behavior and are not forms of punishments.

1. **Related.** The consequence is related to behavior.

2. **Respectful.** It is firmly and kindly enforced to the child, avoiding shame, pain, or blame. The consequence should be respectful to those involved.

3. **Reasonable.** The consequence is seen by the child and by the parent as within the bounds of reason.

4. **Helpful.** It helps to correct misbehavior without inflicting any pain.

For example, the child spills his milk. The **related** consequence is to make him clean it up. A **respectful** remark is, "What do you need to do now?" It is **reasonable** to let him clean up the mess. It will be **helpful** if you will show him how to do it but do not do it for him.

Remember that, if one of the criteria is missing, the consequence is not logical anymore.

C. The 4Rs of Punishment

Eliminating one of the positive criteria of logical consequences will result in negative responses that are embodied in the 4Rs, making the child resent the person who is disciplining him and feel bad.

1. **Resentment**.

"It is unfair." "I cannot trust adults."

2. **Revenge**.

"I will get even."

3. Rebellion.

"I will show them that I can do whatever I want."

4. **Retreat** (or sneakiness).

"I will not let them catch me next time."

Are they effective?

Both are effective strategies because of the following:

- It allows the child to make a choice.

- It is closely-tied to the kid's behavior, giving him lessons when he misbehaves.

- It is concerned with both present and future behavior, training the child to become responsible for his actions.

- It does not punish or shame the child, keeping the deed separated from the doer.

- It is done in a calm environment, making him feel secure and safe.

To ensure its effectiveness, you must think ahead and prepare a proper response. You should avoid "saving" your child and refrain from stepping in. Allowing him to experience the consequence will teach him vital lessons. If the consequence does not work during the first enforcement, keep putting it into action until it resolves the problem.

Helpful tips to effectively use Natural and Logical consequences:

1. Identifying the reasons.

For every action, there is a reason. Same goes when your child misbehaves. It is possible that he wants to get your complete attention, get even, gain control or power, or feel inadequate.

- Paying no attention is one classic example of getting attention, and gaining power over adults. Say, your child is playing and you give him 5 minutes to finish and put his toy away. Even if you say "one-minute left," he keeps on playing and having fun. Now, all your attention is on him.

2. Deciding whose problem it is.

Let your child faces his own problem. Do not interfere, as long as the consequences will not harm his safety or health.

- If it begins to rain and your kid does not heed your warning that playtime is up, he might get drenched. This is a natural consequence.

- If he does not put the toys away, it can be your problem because leaving them outside is not safe because someone might get it if. If you are training him to become more responsible by bringing back his toys inside your house, and he refuses to do it, you can use a logical consequence.

3. Offering choices or alternatives.

Keep in mind that logical consequence is the result of your child's choice. Offer safe, positive, and limited choices that will prompt him to behave accordingly or do something about the problem.

- Tell your kid, "You need to pick your toys now. If you leave them outside, you are not allowed to play them tomorrow. It's your choice."

4. Being firm.

After he makes a choice, you need to follow through the consequence. Do not waver, show him that you are serious about enforcing the rule. If you slip even once, the child knows that he can get past the logical consequence and will attempt to do it again.

- Say, *"All right then, I can see that you do not want to play with your toys tomorrow."* Pick up the toys and store them away, where he cannot reach them. Most probably, your child will cry and throw fits, just be calm, and remind him that he already made a choice.

5. Talking about choices in a positive way.

Giving choices is more appealing to your children compared to a warning. Though the logical consequence may be similar, by being positive instead of threatening, you prevent power struggles.

- Maybe if you rephrase your words, he will show cooperation. "I want you to play with your toys tomorrow, so let's pick them up and bring inside, so they will not disappear like your favorite ball which you left it here."

6. Letting the child know if he had done something good.

As soon as you see your child correcting his behavior and doing what is appropriate, acknowledge it. Avoid over-praising, simply say it's great. It will reinforce his motivation to meet your expectations and follow the rules.

- If the next day, you see your child picking up his toys and putting them in proper storage even if you do not remind him, say *"Wow, I can see that you are taking care of your toys. I am proud of you!"*

7. Involving your child when deciding on the consequences.

Because it primarily involves the child, and he is the one who will suffer the consequences of his behavior and choices, ask suggestions from him.

- Initiate a conversation with your child and discuss what will happen if he does not bring in the toys after playing. He will probably say that other children might get them. Then, you can say that toys cost money and if they are lost, it would not be possible to buy toys for him. Maybe he would answer that he might be able to help you buy new toys because he has savings. In the end, you both agreed that the best solution is for him to pick them up after playing in the outdoors.

When imposing logical consequences to young children (8 years old and below), remember the following:

- **Calm down**. Step back for a while, take a deep breath, and control impulses to yell or punish the child.

- **Don't be a bully.** Rein your anger because it carries a threat of violence to a child, like the monsters in fairy tales.

- **Stay connected and present**. Do not leave him alone when he is misbehaving. Timeouts may be useful for some time, but it is important for the child not to be left alone for long, or he will feel neglected during times that he is out of control. Wait for him to calm down.

- **Look for appropriate logical consequence**. Use a consequence that is age-appropriate and will make him feel valued, listened to, understood, and respected.

- **Be private**. Always deal with the situation privately. Avoid embarrassing your child by publicly punishing or correcting him.

- **Move on**. After the consequence is over or the time for it has been served, refrain from asking more apologies or lecturing about the behavior. You may gently ask him what he learns from the experience and then allows him to go back to his routine, hoping in your heart that he learned a lesson and will not repeat the act.

CHAPTER 7

Focusing on Solutions

Focusing on solutions that demonstrate respectful, reasonable, helpful, and problem-related is the best approach to resolve misbehavior. It is one of the foundations of successful family meetings, where children are involved in the process of establishing rules and consequences for behavioral issues.

Communication is a vital key to find solutions. A positive and healthy two-way communication is vital to building his self-esteem and self-discipline. Children naturally thrive with praise and words of encouragement, but listening to them boosts their belief in themselves and makes them feel loved and worthy.

A. Positive Communication

Hearing the child utters his first word is a delightful moment for parents. You anticipate the next words and phrases that he is going to say, feeling proud every time he calls you mom or dad. As your child grows, his language development and communication skills evolve. He learns to express his needs, feelings, and thoughts.

Communicating with a baby

The baby's brain is naturally "hard-wired" to the sound of a human voice. He responds using his body language, facial expressions, and noises. To encourage his language development, you need to understand and listen to what he wants to express:

- **Crying**. It is his primary method of communication.

- **Attend to his needs** when he begins to cry, to let him know that you understand and acknowledge his message.

- **Talk** to him frequently about anything or read baby books. He loves hearing your voice and having your presence.

- **Listen** to his noise-making or cooing. Look him in the eye and encourage him to smile or talk.

Communicating with a toddler

Toddlers begin to string words and utter simple sentences using his more than a hundred vocabulary words. Encourage your child's language development with the following:

- Answer his questions using simple language.

- Allow him to finish what he wants to say.

- Spend some time every day just talking with him.

- Listen attentively to what he is saying, instead of correcting his grammar.

- Avoid showing impatient body languages like foot-tapping, sighing, or eye-rolling. It will discourage him from sharing his feelings or thoughts.

- Squat down on his level and maintain eye contact.

- Refrain from talking with him when you are walking away, or your back is turned.

- Smile.

- Cuddle him often.

- Use a gentle tone of voice. Avoid yelling.

- Become aware that if the child is constantly interrupting adult conversations, he wants attention.

Communicating with older children

At this level, he has mastered his language ability and can convey clear ideas. He can alter his speech from casual to formal, depending on the circumstances and interactions. You can show your interest in what he wants to tell you by:

- Making time to listen to your child every day without any distractions. Have an exclusive, quality time with him to talk about anything that concerns him or just random topics that interest you both.

- Respect his point of view and encourage him to give a different opinion.

- Avoid lecturing, criticizing, or interrupting when he is telling you something.

- Ask open-ended questions that will prompt him to share and describe his experiences for the day.

Positive Phrases for Young Children

- Thanks for helping

- You did it!

- I like playing with you

- You are so thoughtful

- Good job

- That was a great try

- Nice idea!

- I am very proud of you

Establishing an open, healthy, and positive communication in the family is empowering. It allows everyone, especially kids, to learn to listen and talk effectively. It is an essential key element of positive parenting, allowing children to express their concerns freely, without criticism and contempt.

Moreover, positive communication is the key to help you and child focus on finding solutions that will make his journey to adulthood an easier and more fulfilling. Helping your child understand, process, manage, and resolve conflict is a life skill, which becomes handy and useful in his everyday life.

It is essential to keep communication positive. How you respond creates immediate impact and affect his mood. For instance, your child will start schooling, and you want him to be prepared mentally and emotionally, so you start sharing some tips and reminders. If you convey that school is fun and exciting because he can play and learn, meet new friends, and more, he will look forward to it. But if you project fears on him, the child will not be too keen to go to school and have a harder time to adjust to the new experience.

Ways to Build-up the Child's Self-esteem:

- Use the words happy and encouraged regularly. *"I feel very encouraged when you extend help to your brother." "I feel happy when you help me."*

- For every negative, always accompany it with at least 3 positives.

- Speak to your kid as you would speak to adults.

- Use the sandwich approach when giving feedback.

- Notice when he is good using specific praise to reinforce the positive behavior.

- Let him know that you believe in his abilities.

- Praise the efforts and not just the results.

- Separate him from his behavior. Show that you disapprove the act, but not him. Say, "drawing on the wall is a naughty thing to do" rather than "you are such a naughty kid."

- Thank him when he helps you and initiates to do household chores.

- Tell your kid what you do want him to do instead of what you don't want.

- Never assume that he already knows how much you love him, tell him often.

The Problem-Solving Approach

1. Talk about the child's feelings and needs.

"I see that you are mad. Is it because your brother took your ball without asking you?"

These statements convey that you know your child's feelings even though he does not say aloud. When you identify and recognize his feelings and needs, you are demonstrating that you understand why he is acting like that or why his behavior has changed.

Always remember to begin all corrections by reaffirming the connection. When children misbehave, they feel bad about the situation or themselves, so they disconnect. To reconnect, you can try these examples:

- Stoop down to his level and look him straight in the eye. *"Pushing hurts, so no pushing. You can tell your brother, "Move, please."*

- Make loving eye contact and say — *"You are upset."*

- Pick him up — *"You want to play longer, but it is time to sleep."*

- Put your hand on his shoulder — *"You are afraid to tell me about the broken vase."*

As a parent, it is your role to help your kid understand his feelings and needs. He needs you to show him how to manage his feelings in constructive and positive ways. Use age-appropriate language and get down to his eye level during the conversation. It shows respect and sincerity, which lets down his guard and become more communicative of his needs and feelings.

Kids, like adults, have their own share of complex feelings that excite, frighten, worry, or make him nervous, embarrassed, or jealous. But it is more difficult for them to express their feelings clearly because they have a limited vocabulary. So, they use other means to communicate with adults like facial expressions, body language, or misbehaviors. When their parents or caregivers cannot decipher what they want to communicate, children display inappropriate acts.

It is important to let your child know that you heard him loud and clear.

- Set a regular talk time and make sure that you give undivided attention to him during the conversation.

- Encourage him to share his feelings, thoughts, fears, dreams, and concerns.

- Guide him to identify and express his feelings, resist the urge to cut in or make his ill feelings go away. Wait until he is ready to talk about possible solutions.

Children who know how to express and cope with their changing emotions are more likely to display the following:

- More supportive and empathetic to others

- Perform better in school and career when they mature

- Have better mental health and wellbeing

- Have more stable, loving, and positive relationships

- Feel more confident, competent, and capable

- Display less behavioral problems

- Have a positive self-concept

- Develop coping skills and resiliency

Teach your older kid to express his frustration, anger, and other strong emotions by:

- Taking some deep breaths

- Taking time out or walking away

- Taking time to relax, then try again

- Saying what he feels rather than acting it out

- Finding another way to do things

- Asking for support or assistance

- Trying to solve problems with words

- Spending time with you or asking for a cuddle/hug

2. Talk about your feelings and needs.

"I am sad that you and your brother quarreled."

By telling your child what you feel, you are sending him a message that you do not like him and his sibling quarreling over a toy. And you also expect him to be more tolerant and generous because he is the older one.

It is okay to express your feelings and needs in a way that is clear and does not shame your kid. If you are angry, it is much better to wait until you regain your self-control and talk to him later. Never discipline or problem-solve when you are angry. As a parent, you are the model of the behaviors you want him to acquire. How you respond and handle the conflict impacts the way he responds.

Parenting is a difficult job, which sometimes brings out natural reactions. But remember, that just like your child, you are human and prone to stress, anxiety, and other negative emotions. If you are unhappy, stressed, or worried, it is extremely hard to be objective or handle the situations that involve your child. So, do not underestimate the importance of keeping yourself healthy and in top condition. It is important to take care of your well-being while taking care of your family. Have realistic expectations- for yourself, kids, and spouse. You are not superhuman, and you don't have all the answers. If you need help, talk to your family, friends, and other support systems.

Your child will also appreciate you being open to him, in terms of your own feelings and needs. Share your own childhood experiences and lessons learned. Sharing personal stories will help him see you in a better light, that once upon a time, you were a child like him. Use the opportunity to let him know you better, not just as a mom or dad, but someone who has gone through different experiences.

3. Brainstorm together and find a mutually agreeable solution to the conflict.

Sit down and discuss the problem with your child when both of you have calmed down. You can use these simple steps:

1. **Show empathy and concern**. Using a non-accusing, gentle tone, acknowledge your concern for what happened. Avoid making a long lecture. Simply state what you see or observe.

"It looks like you and your brother want the same ball, but it is not good to fight."

2. **Define the problem**. Briefly explain why quarreling is not good, especially between siblings. Give emphasis on why it should not happen again and why it is important to change the behavior. Use the "When and then" approach to emphasize the impact of the misbehavior. *"When you hit your brother or other people, he feels hurt and sad. Do you want that to happen?"*

3. **Ask for ideas**. *"What will you do about it?" or "Let's think about ways to prevent it."*

4. Record all the ideas, without evaluating.

Get a pen and paper, then write down all the solutions that you both think. Listen to his ideas and practical solutions.

5. Decide and agree on a mutually-acceptable, feasible solution.

Categorize all the answers into three sections- ideas you both like, don't like and plan to follow through. Then, review the best suggestions and decide together.

B. Using encouragement effectively

Encouragement, when used properly, bring positive effects, but indiscriminate or overusing it brings the opposite and do more harm to the kid instead of good.

Encouragement vs. Praise

Encouragement points out specific facts without evaluating them. It is non-judgmental. Examples are "I know that you work hard to finish your project" or "Look at those pretty details in your painting." These examples point out certain things that were highlighted in his performance, but you did not evaluate them. The encouraging words you say develop a sense of pride and enhance his motivation to do better the next time around.

Praise focuses on what parents (adults) feel or think. It often uses judgment like good, nice, best, and so on. For example, "You are such a nice boy." "I like that you are a very good dancer." Sometimes, kids who receive a lot of praise do things to please adults and not because they want to do them.

Yes, it is necessary for children to receive praise or reinforcement, but encouragement is far more powerful when you are disciplining your child, helping him build his self-concept, teaching him values, and motivating him to cooperate. So, when you are about to say "You're a great boy!", change it to "You share your toys with your playmate. Thank you for being generous." This will encourage him to be more generous, compassionate, and proud of his accomplishments.

Other benefits that encouragement brings:

- It increases the intrinsic motivation
- It enhances perseverance

- It improves self-esteem and self-confidence

- It sets up children for future success

The key to using encouragement effectively is knowing **when** and **how** to express it.

1. **Be sincere and honest.** Say encouraging words that are consistent with the facts.

- *Say- "Well done! You did well in your test. Keep up the good work!"*

- *Don't use overly effusive or general words like "You're a genius, I am sure that you will do great again next time!"*

2. **Be descriptive and specific**. Refrain from using sweeping statements or comments, which can be perceived as not factually correct. The better way is to point out a specific behavior or skill that helps him perform well. It shows that you really paid attention to his performance and you really care.

- *Say- "You picked up the right colors for your painting project."*

- *Don't say — "Good job on that one!" or "That was awesome!"*

3. **Focus on the effort and the process, rather than ability.** When you attribute your child's achievement to the effort he exerted, he will be motivated to improve his skills through practice. It leads to a growth mindset that increases his persistence, motivation, and enjoyment to master his craft.

On the other hand, a child who is praised for his ability instead of his efforts will also be motivated to try harder and succeed. However, most often than not, children in the praised domain quit faster when they face failure. They suffer from an achievement-based concept that makes them more vulnerable.

- *Say- "Your strategy was excellent!"*

- *Don't say — "Your ability to solve the problem is excellent!"*

4. **Avoid Comparison.** A comparison can be double-edged. It can be motivating or can be depressing for children, leaving them vulnerable to setbacks.

- *Say — "Your great focus helped you solve the problem."*

- *Don't say – "You are smarter than your brother."*

5. **Avoid handing out too many encouraging words for easy tasks**. It may lead children to avoid complex tasks, and select those that are easy to complete. It also implies that there is originally a lower expectation of competence and parents are over-handing words as an extrinsic reward which lessens, not increases motivation. When it is not given, kids may think that the absence of praise signifies failure. Furthermore, giving it indiscriminately may lead to an over-inflated self-image that develops narcissistic children or constant pressure to outperform the previous performance.

It may give an idea that he is valued because he met the standards, but what if he fails? Does it mean that he is a failure?

Other motivating ways to encourage your kid:

- **Have fun together**. Allow the child to select a task and do it together, like washing the car or cleaning the yard. The goal is to have fun.

- **Have a regular conversation**. Talk about various topics that interest you and your child is another meaningful activity. The goal is to understand each other better.

- **Listen to your child**. Be willing to listen when he calls your attention. It makes him feel important and subsequently, learn to express his feelings with clarity. The goal is to help your child become more confident and open to share his experiences.

- **Show your love, no matter what**. The most valuable words that your child wants to hear during his down moments like failing to get high grades or make it to the sports team is "I love you." Appreciating his efforts at the moment of sadness is also vital because it will encourage him to do better the next time. The goal is to show that no matter what happens, you are there to support and love him.

- **Admit when you are mistaken and say sorry.** When you are wrong, it's okay to apologize to your child. It conveys that they are not perfect and commit mistakes sometimes. The goal is to teach your child to become responsible for his thoughts and actions and learn to apologize when he is wrong.

- **Exhibit his achievements prominently**. Displaying his trophies, medals, and other proofs of achievement at home encourage the child to accomplish more and be more hardworking. This will make him more receptive to try new things and accept new challenges. The goal is to make him see you proud even without saying them aloud all the time.

- **Create a nostalgic activity**. One fun way is to review his previous years of accomplishments like certificates, art and crafts, projects, pictures, and stories together. Talk about his happy experiences during those winning moments. The goal is to l encourage and motivate him to keep doing better.

- **Provide responsibility**. Allow your child to do simple household chores like preparing his favorite meal, picking up trash, or feeding the pets. The goal is to make him feel more capable, responsible, and in control of his world, encouraging him to aspire for bigger things in life.

- **Let him know that he did a good job**. Let him know that you appreciate his efforts by giving a thumbs up, hugging, or treating him with ice cream. Simple gestures like these are more meaningful compared to lavish praises. The goal is to motivate him to keep up doing his best in everything he pursues.

C. How your personality affects your kid?

Anecdotal evidence in various studies on parenting revealed that the dominant personality traits of parents create deep impact and induce large ripple effects on children. What he believes, feels, and thinks are impressions of his observations and experiences at home, in particular, the personalities of his parents. He mirrors their traits and reflects them in terms of academic performance, effectiveness to handle tasks, and harmonious social interactions.

Your personality is the strongest force that affects your child's own personality, not to mention the inherited genes. If you have a positive personality that displays healthy characteristics, virtues, wisdom, and maturity, it is more likely that your child will mirror your traits. He will also reflect positivity, happiness, and sincerity in his life, becoming more competent in facing multiple life domains if you are a positive individual.

The two core dimensions of parenting that affect children are warmth and hostility.

- **Parental warmth** refers to the general tendency to be affectionate, supportive, and sensitive to your child's needs. It promotes the kid's pro-social behavior by giving him a sense of security, trust, and control of the environment. Accordingly, it predicts the positive development of better academic engagement and performance, along with adaptive coping strategies that secure attachment and good behavior.

- **Hostility** or coercive parenting behavior is an inhibitor of pro-social development. It promotes risk factors such as coercion and harshness that may lead to behavioral issues that are linked with kids' aggressive and oppositional behavior.

It leads to the observations that the parent's personality has a direct and mediation link with the personality of a child, in particular during adolescence.

Eric Berne's Transactional Analysis is one of the most popular theories that delve on the effects of parents' personality in the development of children's personality and behavior. According to his theory, every single person has recordings in the brain which shape the personality. They are also called impressions or imprints that come from childhood observations and classified into three:

5. **Impressions that show the sense of right and wrong, norms, rules, or moral duties**- They inspire people to be compassionate, helpful, and nurturing. Berne described them as the outcomes of observing the behavior of parents or imbibing parental teachings. He labeled these impressions as "Parent" or "P", saying that everyone has impressions of a Nurturing Parent or a Controlling Parent in their brain.

6. **Impressions that come from own experiences and acts**- Whenever you do something active and get good results, you gather new insights which develop your understanding about life and the world in general. Berne called these impressions as "Adult" or "A".

7. **Impressions as outcomes of natural reactions to different situations**- They form the spontaneous aspect of personality and are tagged as "Child" or "C".

These recordings significantly impact an individual's personality. Children with lots of impressions of a Nurturing

Parent grow up as affectionate and caring adults, while those with records of Controlling Parents are most likely to have commanding personalities.

CHAPTER 8

Support

At this juncture, it is vital to reinforce the objectives of Positive Discipline, remembering that it is about teaching essential life and social skills in manners that are encouraging and respectful to both the learners (children) and mentors (parents, teachers, caregivers, childcare providers). It is based on the concept that discipline must be taught to children with kindness and firmness, neither permissive nor punitive.

To make Positive Discipline more effective, it is necessary for parents, teachers, and other adult influences to create a nurturing environment that meets all the basic needs of the child such as food, shelter, and clothing, extending to non-physical needs such as love, encouragement, and acceptance.

- **Parental love** is about the unconditional love that is acted out by providing care and gentle guidance, giving time and attention to children, and helping them resolve any social conflict.

- **Acceptance** is making children feel that no matter what they do, whether wrong or right, they are loved.

- **Encouragement** is showing support in concrete ways that help children figure out how to avoid or correct mistakes, including finding their strengths to pursue passions and life goals.

In a nutshell, parents are the major support of children who ensure their positive growth and development.

A. Positive Discipline at Home

Discipline begins at home. As early as possible, kids are taught to be responsible for their actions and distinguish what is right from wrong. Positive Discipline at home uses healthy and positive interactions that aim to prevent inappropriate acts or behavioral problems before they begin and become habits. It teaches kids the correct behavior and be respectful through appreciation, encouragement, consequences, and other non-violent strategies.

The outcomes are:

- Children do better when there is routine, consistency, and lots of positive encouragement.

- A positive relationship with parents greatly reduces the occurrence of challenging behavior.

- A non-punitive discipline that provides effective long-term benefits compared to punishment.

- Children respond positively to parents or caregivers whom they trust.

To be most effective, it is important to use the strategies consistently by all caregivers.

1. *Creating a safe environment*

Childproof your home and supervise his movements at all times to see that he is safe while exploring his immediate surroundings.

2. *Establishing a routine*

Routines help children perform or behave properly because they know the expectations of their parents. A specific routine that guarantees his optimum care, safety, and enjoyment will help your child feel secure, more in control, and less anxious, hence developing strong self-discipline.

3. *Planning ahead*

If you have to run errands and need to take your child with you, it is necessary to talk to him and let him know of your expectations on his behaviors. This will prepare him and try his best to behave well. However, for little children who do not fully comprehend yet what you are trying to say, better have toys, crayons, books, and other activity tools with you when you go out to keep him occupied while shopping, waiting for the doctor's appointment, or traveling.

4. Having clear expectations

Discuss your expectation with your child. If you set 5 expectations like- Be Kind, Be Respectful, Be Responsible, Be Helpful, and Be Safe, do not forget to tell them. Have a conversation with him about the acts and deeds that demonstrate your expectations. Make sure that you also display those acceptable behaviors because your child is always watching your examples.

5. Offering choices

Choices that are suitable for his age will help him gain a sense of independence and self-control. By offering choices, you are empowering him to become more decisive and stand up for what he believes is right for him. It also applies to the consequences of misbehavior or disobeying your rules. Make him choose between two safe, logical consequences, which aim to give him a lesson and a warning not to repeat the mistake again. Always follow through and enforce the consequence to make him see that you are really serious about discipline.

6.   Building a positive relationship

Spending quality time with your child reinforces your relationship, helping him develop a strong sense of belonging, significance, and connection. Allow him to choose the activity or topic. It also lessens the occurrence of misbehavior because he does not want to disappoint you.

7.   Redirecting the negative behavior

Maybe your child is bored, or for whatever reason, he starts acting out. It is important to provide a good alternative that will stop him from misbehaving and enjoy himself. Always make sure that your child is well-rested, well-fed, and engaged in stimulating and fun activity. Redirecting his sudden negative behavior to another activity that interests him will generate appropriate behavior.

8.   Calm down before you address misbehavior

Never try to discipline your child when you are angry, frustrated, or experiencing physical or mental fatigue because you will lose your objectivity. Calm yourself first and take a time out to steady your nerves. This will help you think clearly and handle the situation fairly, yet firmly.

9. Being firm and kind at the same time

This is the positive discipline in its best form. You respond to each situation or misbehavior with kindness and respect to your child, but firm enough to impose the consequences. It is also important to let your child explain and justify his acts, but no matter how convincing his reason, make him understand that rules are rules. Remind him that you set limits for a purpose- to keep him safe and prevent mistakes that may hurt him or others. If he chooses to defy any of them, he needs to face the consequences of his actions.

10. Catch him being good

Do not let good deeds go unnoticed. Whenever you observe your child behaving properly, appreciate his efforts, so he is aware that he is doing well.

Distinguishing Factors between Normal Behavior and Misbehavior:

How do you know that your child is displaying misbehavior or normal behavior? As a parent, it is necessary to have realistic expectations about the behavior of your kid, taking into consideration the stage of his development. Every stage has distinct challenges that trigger behaviors, which you can mistakenly view as intentional misbehavior. By understanding these stages, you will know the difference.

Here are some examples of normal or developmentally appropriate behavior:

Example No. 1:

- **Developmentally Appropriate or Normal Behavior:** Tantrums

- **Developmental Tasks:** The child is beginning to handle his frustrations and throws tantrums when upset and does not understand why he needs to do something. A classic example is when he does not want to brush his teeth or go to bed early.

Example No. 2:

- **Developmentally Appropriate or Normal Behavior:** Energetic and Active

- **Developmental Tasks:** The need to explore and discover. One manifestation is the difficulty to sit quietly for a long time like during church attendance or storytelling period.

Example No. 3:

- **Developmentally Appropriate or Normal Behavior**: Independent

- **Developmental Tasks**: He wants to do things on his own like feeding himself, choosing clothes to wear, or picking the toys he wants to play.

Example No. 4:

- **Developmentally Appropriate or Normal Behavior**: Being talkative

- **Developmental Tasks:** He becomes extremely curious about everything around him, so he asks a lot of questions. His vocabulary is also growing, so he is excited to use the words he learns.

What to do when your child is misbehaving:

- Stop whatever you are doing and give your full attention to your child.

- Remain calm and speak with your normal voice tone.

- If out in a public area, remove him from the situation that triggers his emotional outburst.

- Get down to his eye level.

- Make him understand what you feel before reminding your child about your expectations from him. *"I know that you still want to play, but it is time to go home."*

- Discuss the expected behavior and asks him what he needs to do about it.

- State the consequence for the misbehavior.

- Follow through with the consequence.

- Acknowledge when you see your child correcting his behavior.

- Reconnect and restore your relationship through affection, hugs, or plays.

Dealing with a little child can be tiring and challenging, so do not forget to take care of yourself. It is a must to find time for yourself and find support when necessary.

- Eat a healthy diet and exercise regularly.

- Spend time in nature or have a "me" time to relax.

- Engage in activities that make you feel good and happy. Do them regularly.

- Keep in touch with family and friends.

- Say no to extra responsibilities.

B. Positive Discipline in Classroom

The Teacher-Student Relationship

Aside from teaching academic lessons, teachers have a responsibility to instill discipline that keeps children well-behaved and avoid inappropriate acts inside the classroom or within the school premises. They need to build a trusting and caring relationship with each student to create a harmonious, conducive, and happy learning environment. The positive achievements of the students reflect the teachers' performance and how they see them as their "role model."

It is necessary to remember that every child is an individual with a different history, different home life experience, different dreams, and different way to respond to situations. By taking the time to get to know them, one by one, and their parents during classroom meetings, teachers show they care and respect their uniqueness.

Students feel valued and safe in a respectful environment, reducing the occurrences of misbehavior. According to the American Academy of Pediatrics, the techniques to lessen or prevent misbehavior among children will only be effective when:

- Both the teacher and student truly understand the problem behavior and the expected consequence of the wrong act.

- The appropriate consequence for misbehavior is enforced consistently each time it happens.

- It provides a reason for the student to learn the lesson of the specific consequence.

- Teachers enforce discipline and consequences in a calm, yet firm manner.

Punishment vs. Positive Discipline in School

- **Punishment** is the action or penalty imposed on the student for breaking a rule or misbehaving. Its impact is detrimental to the child in both physical and emotional aspects. It is not effective in preventing or reducing future occurrences of misbehavior despite the attempt to control the child using verbal disapproval and corporal punishment that usually involves physical or emotional pain.

- **Positive Discipline**, on the other hand, has become a better alternative to punishment. It is the practice of teaching or training students to obey the school rules or code of behavior using a positive approach. Rather than controlling their behaviors, teachers apply positive discipline techniques to help students develop self-control and make positive choices that generate good behaviors. With positive discipline, teacher-student conflict is prevented during behavior skills management. It helps teachers shape students' character by using empowering words of encouragement.

Why Children Misbehave in the Classroom

Students do not misbehave intentionally. There is a cause or a reason for his inappropriate display of emotions. Some of the common reasons are:

- The lesson does not interest him and he is bored.

- The methods of teaching do not fit the learning style of the student.

- The task is too hard or too easy for him.

- The expectations are unreasonable and unclear.

- The student is not prepared.

- The student cannot communicate well, has low self-esteem, or poor social skills.

All these reasons may discourage students. Students who are discouraged usually misbehave. They believe that they do not belong or not useful, thus seeking to belong by displaying misbehavior.

In addition, students also misbehave to attain these four goals:

1. Attention

2. Revenge

3. Avoidance of Failure (Inadequacy)

4. Power

To decode these goals, think about one student that frustrates, irritates, or worries you. To find out the reason behind his misbehavior, you need to ask yourself how you feel whenever the student misbehaves.

- If you feel angry, his goal is to achieve power.

- If you feel annoyed, he wants attention.

- If you feel frustrated, he believes that he is inadequate and cannot measure up to others.

- If you feel hurt, his objective is revenge.

Positive Discipline in the Classroom

It is a comprehensive approach that guides the mentors to instill discipline in such a way that promotes positive student behavior, cooperation, and mutual respect. It provides the necessary tools to create an atmosphere of learning that is conducive to children, motivating them to learn and enjoy the lessons better. This approach teaches students to adapt their behaviors to meet the teacher's expectations and learn to make better choices that will lead them to the path of success. It produces students who think critically and make self-decisions based on good choices.

- Positive Discipline Brings Positive Outcomes

Logically, when you focus on the positive, you attract positive things. Positive discipline works in the same manner inside the classroom. When teachers set high expectations, the students will try to meet them. If they set a low bar, the students will match the expectations without too much effort. A positive approach helps students see their self-worth and capabilities, and they aim to achieve and behave to meet expectations.

- Positive Discipline Teaches Logic

This approach allows teachers to help students learn from their mistakes or correct misbehavior by making them see the cause and effect of their choices. It teaches them the logic and reasoning behind every action, prompting them to choose what is right and proper to avoid consequences.

- Positive Discipline Focuses on Students Behavior, Not Who They Are

Positive discipline has a language that helps students review their actions and behaviors. Teachers do not use the word "bad," instead "the action is not a good choice." By practicing this strategy, you are giving the student a chance to modify his behavior or choice and feel good.

Positive Discipline Techniques

There are effective positive discipline techniques that create and support an inclusive teaching-learning environment. Teachers must work hand in hand with parents and students to ensure the success of the Positive Discipline program. One crucial aspect of positive discipline in the classroom is to teach students new positive behaviors that meet the expectations at home, classroom, and anywhere they go.

Here are some of the strategies:

- Establishing the classroom rules at the beginning of the school year.

- Set fair and consistent expectations.

- Create goals for the whole year.

- Make individual plans for students.

- Provide students with various choices.

- Model appropriate behaviors.

- Ensure that appropriate behaviors are reinforced.

- Use praise (but not lavishly)

- Student dignity matters at all times

- Find the root cause of the misbehavior

- Remain neutral during students' conflicts

- Listen to students

- Remove objects in the classroom that cause distractions

Benefits of Positive Discipline in the Classroom

The positive techniques of this type of discipline help teachers resolve and overcome challenges in the classroom while helping the students make better choices that prepare them in their mature years. The strategies allow the mentors to create a classroom environment where students are encouraged to resolve their friendship/classmate issues to reduce or prevent power struggles and gain a sense of value and connection.

Positive discipline also brings the following benefits:

- Increases academic success

- Reduces disciplinary measures

- Attendance improves

- Fewer expulsions and suspensions

- Students display greater respect

- Students are actively engaged in tasks

The benefits extend beyond the four corners of the classroom, into the social environment, sports, home life, and elsewhere.

Preventive Measures

One aspect of positive discipline is preventing situations that trigger negative behaviors. The teacher needs to see each kid as an account, where she needs to deposit positive experiences before she can withdraw. Deposits are in the form of encouragement, smiles, fun classroom activities, special tasks, appropriate pat on the back, and simple acts that boost their self-worth.

Most children long for attention, and if they did not receive it, they tend to exhibit misbehavior to attract negative attention. For them, it may be negative, and they may face certain consequences, but they get what they want.

- In handling a student who does not know what appropriate behavior he should display, the teacher can teach him. For instance, one of her students is fighting over a toy in such a dramatic way that distracts everyone in the room. To create a fair solution, she needs to approach them and talk about the problem, encouraging the misbehaving child to give input about the right way to borrow the toy and avoid future arguments with his classmates.

- For students who feel unaccepted or unwanted, the teacher should first develop trust between them before she can instill proper discipline.

- The teacher should recognize students who do not get along well together and separate them from the beginning to prevent situations that may trigger negative behaviors. Hence, it is important to employ girl-boy-girl-boy method of circling or lining up, as well as arrange the classroom in a way that is conducive to optimum learning and discipline. To encourage her students to make new friends, she can also separate groups of friends while in the classroom.

- As much as possible, the rules are devised by children, with the help of the authority figure and agreed upon by the involved parties. Teachers can make suggestions and discussed them during group meetings where everyone present has equal rights to vote for or against the rules and give input. By involving children in creating rules and approving them, they become more accountable responsible.

- Be explicit about the rules, expectations, and consequences. Students who clearly understand are more compliant and responsible. All consequences should be delivered in a firm, yet kind manner to preserve mutual respect and trust between the teacher and the student.

- The teacher should use positive recognition, which rewards good behavior and curtails negative ones through "verbal" rewards or actual gifts. She may say, "I like the way you help Crystal find her book" or "Thank you, Chris, for joining the line." The teacher can also employ a reward system like giving stamps in the notebook for completing lessons. Each stamp is a credit, and when they earn a certain total like 50-100, they receive certificates. Other forms of positive recognition are giving out high fives and words of encouragement, a special necklace that is passed from one student to another for doing a good deed, and displaying awards on the classroom achievement wall.

Positive Discipline Tools for Teachers

1. *Family Chores and Classroom Jobs* – This tool encourages students to contribute in meaningful ways, making them learn the value of the contribution. It fosters the natural inclination to help.

2. *Connection Before Correction* – It teaches the concept that brainstorming solutions and working together to solve the problem become easier when everyone is calm and connected.

- **Connection**- "I care about what are telling me." (Verbalize care)

- **Correction**– "Let us sit down and brainstorm solutions that will be acceptable to everyone."

- **Connection**- "I can see that you are angry and disappointed." (Validate feeling)

- **Correction** – "It's okay to feel angry, but it's not okay to kick. Anything else you can do?

3. *Class Meetings*- They promote overall connection, give children a sense of belonging, allowing them to contribute input, and practice their problem-solving skills. All concerns are on the agenda, and everyone works to address issues and find long-term solutions. Positive Discipline provides teachers/parents specific meeting format that aims to help children learn through brainstorming and discussion of possible solutions. Moreover, they learn to be compassionate and show concern for others as well as how to learn from their mistakes and become accountable for their actions.

3. *Asking Curiosity Questions*- Positive Discipline encourages adults to refrain from using commands that incite acts of rebellion and resistance. Instead, it advocates asking questions that invite cooperation and feeling of capability. Examples of simple questions that will motivate kids to look for solutions are:

- What do you need to wear so you won't be cold when you go outside?

- What is your plan for completing your school project?

- How can you and your sister solve the problem together?

- What are your plans for cleaning your room?

Positive Discipline fails if:

- *The teacher puts emphasis on the tasks instead of behaviors.*

    o **Don't say** - *"It's nice you stopped talking."*

    o **Do say**– *"It's nice you were considerate of your classmates and quieted down quickly."*

- The student/class is not rewarded (verbal or simple gifts) quickly.

- The emphasis is on what the student is doing incorrectly, instead of appropriate or correct deeds.

C. Love and Joy in Homes and Classrooms

What makes Positive Discipline an ideal tool for parents and classroom teachers is, it is geared to creating a loving and joyful environment. It enables children and adults to experience more love, joy, mutual respect, harmony, cooperation, responsibility, and a lot more positive things in life. Most people forget that life is more wonderful when you share love and joy with family. Teaching becomes easier and more conducive to learning when there are joy and love in the classroom.

Remember this classic joke?

After his first day at school, the mother asked his child, "What did you learn at school today?" The child replied, "Not enough Mom, I have to go back tomorrow."

Joy and love are essential to a healthy climate. A joyful and embracing classroom environment induces better assimilation of knowledge, develops social skills, lessens stress, and makes children look forward to another day of a learning experience.

In the context of Positive Discipline, there are three reminders that remind adults, not to make detours that curtail the experience of having a loving, joyful, and satisfying relationship with children.

1. What You Do is Not as Important as How You Do It

Your attitude and feeling on everything you do determine the "how" of your actions. The emotions you feel become evident in the tone of your voice. Voicing out your negative feelings and thoughts can drive away love and joy, attracting negative outcomes and destroying relationships.

2. View Mistakes as Learning Opportunities

Adults should see every misbehavior or mistakes of children as an opportunity to teach positive discipline, using the principles that maintain respect, love, joy, trust, and gain positive results.

3. Learn the Same Thing Over and Over

"How many times do I have to tell you?", this is a familiar statement that parents and teachers use. It is important to remember that your child does not quite understand or completely comprehend what you are telling him, so you need to be patient and continue teaching or training him.

Cultivating Love & Joy at Homes

- **Accept imperfections.** Your child will make mistakes as he grows. It is more important to focus on helping him master the skills in problem-solving and making good choices. Practice forgiveness, acceptance, and compassion, traits that you like your child to imitate.

- **Listen.** Foster connection by tuning into your kid's dreams, joys, fears, hopes, and heartaches. Sometimes, you just need to listen and show support and not worry about fixing anything. Ask creative and fun questions to start a conversation and allow your child to spill out his inner feelings.

- **Smile and Laugh**. These simple acts generate joy and loving atmosphere at home. They are so simple, yet so very powerful and contagious.

- **Encourage**. Learn to celebrate every success, process and progress, courage, and determination in simple ways. Embrace both failure and success with unconditional love and support. Appreciate the efforts that your child exerted. Encouragement helps in the development of resiliency and growth mindset, motivating your child to study harder, try harder, and become better.

- **Dare to Be Ridiculous**. Have fun together, dance, create, play, invent, or whatever you and your child enjoy doing. Step out of your comfort zone and unleash your inner child again by joining your kid in his favorite game or sport.

- **Spend time together**. Look for an opportunity to spend time with your child every day, even for a short period and use it to truly connect with him. You can make snacks together, reading a new book, play a game after finishing homework, go grocery shopping, or just talk about his day in school.

- **Choose love**. Life can be challenging, complicated, or stressful, but always choose love to dwell inside your house. Strive to become the source of love for your child, giving him support and loving guidance.

- **Say it**. Express your love for your child at least once a day with "I love you."

- **Give lots of kisses and hugs**. Physical touch strengthens the bond with your child and to the development of emotions.

- **Be available for your child**. Have time to answer his questions, play, teach, dry his tears, calm his fears, or cheer him on.

- **Make your home a safe refuge**. A home where love and joy dwell unconditionally makes the child feel secure against the cruel world.

- **Keep your kid safe**. Childproof the house. Do not leave him with someone who is uncaring and not worthy to be around him. Protection is a manifestation of love.

- **Raise them to be capable and independent**. Allow your kids to go out and explore the world. Holding them too tight is not love-it is selfishness.

- **Be lovable**. Cultivate joy in your heart and express it without reservation. Love yourself and others. Have fun alone and with others.

Cultivating Love & Joy in the Classrooms

No strategy, method, or technique can motivate students more than a joyful classroom, where love and concern for each other are freely-given. A nurturing classroom environment makes the children focus on their academic tasks, be more attentive, and well-mannered.

Teachers, as second parents, have a big responsibility to instill love and joy in her students, which can effectively inspire and encourage them to attend schools and learn. Without joy and love, there will instance of misbehavior and disrespect. Students will be bored and dissatisfied and do not look forward to engaging with classmates or listening to your lectures. Disciplining them becomes more challenging, too.

Good thing, creating a joyful classroom is easy. It does require extra planning, great sacrifice, or a big budget. It just requires YOU – your actions, attitudes, body language, tone of voice, and smile. It needs your enthusiasm to teach, to impart knowledge, and mold children to become productive members of society.

- Be well-prepared every day-physically, emotionally, and mentally.

- Focus on the acts of teaching, on your students, and on creating motivating learning experiences.

Here are some ways teachers cultivate a happy learning environment:

- Create a "Daily News" where students share their best moment in the morning, before the actual lesson. You can level it up by recording the child's moments and creating a simple newsletter which they can take home and show to their parents. You need a classroom helper or paraprofessional to type the shared experiences of the students. Make the newsletter exciting with images that depict joy, love, and happiness.

- Share a note. You can write simple notes or draw simple images on index cards or Post-Its, with words of encouragement, specific praise, or gratitude. For instance, *"Your comment about our topic today is thoughtful and smart"* or *"I love the way you show your classmate the proper way to solve the problem."* These messages of love will boost their self-esteem and motivation. You can also ask them to write notes to their parents or each other.

- Use the power of the Internet and create a blog where students can share their happy moments and discoveries.

- Share love beyond the classroom by organizing social action projects to develop their sense of compassion, volunteerism, cooperation, and teamwork.

Ways to Encourage Positive Student Behaviors

- **Provide attention** to increase positive behavior inside and outside the classroom.

- **Provide consistency** by establishing regular routines of interactions and activities every day.

- **Build confidence** by promoting positive self-talk. Ask your students to share what they think are their strengths or positive trait. Apply their answers to your lesson.

- **Respond consistently** to positive and negative behavioral situations to foster harmonious student-teacher relationship and bring positive performance outcomes.

- **Be flexible,** especially with adolescent or older child. Listen to his reasons for misbehavior or for not complying. It shows that you care about his viewpoint and understand, but firm to enforce the necessary consequence of his actions. Involve your students during decision-making on rules, limits, or consequences that are geared to attain long-term results.

- **Make learning more meaningful and interesting** by modifying your instructional methods and utilizing fun activities.

By cultivating love and joy, everything else follows.

Everyday Solutions to Parenting Problems

Parenting is both a science and art, bringing out your creative juices while encouraging you to be open-minded about the growth phases that your child goes through.

The **science of parenting** is applying what is good and safe for children. It is about searching to find results and answers which you can replicate day after day. It is a science because you and your child are both biological entities. Parenting involves the knowledge of psychology, anthropology, sociology, genetics, and nutrition, such as:

- The knowledge that when babies sleep on the stomach may lead to sudden infant death syndrome (SIDS) because sleeping down may cause rebreathing exhaled carbon dioxide, so you make you sure that he sleeps on his back.

- Breastfeeding is the best way to feed your child, so you opt to breastfeed him.

- Excessive crying is highly-dangerous, so you immediately respond when he cries.

The **art of parenting** is responding creatively in nurturing and disciplining children. Being a parent is about finding and developing your strategies to build a strong relationship with the child while enforcing loving guidance or Positive Discipline.

- It is about inculcating family values to make him a well-rounded individual.

- It is finding ways to sneak vegetables to his favorite meal.

- It is about seeing his world, from many different perspectives.

- It is about allowing your child to explore the environment and discover things in a trial and error method.

- It is learning to trust your instincts and seeing every experience as an opportunity for you and your child.

Stage by Stage Effective & Healthy Discipline Tips

A. Infants

- Your child learns by watching you, so set a good example by demonstrating nice behaviors.

- Teach him to learn how to self-soothe by not brushing off or ignoring his needs. Comfort him when upset, sick, or hurt.

- He needs consistent discipline, so set rules for everyone to follow (spouse, caregiver, and other family members).

- Use positive language when communicating with your child. Instead of "Don't stand", use "Time to sit."

- Limit the use of the word "No". Use it only to ensure safety and other important issues.

B. Toddlers

- Your kid is beginning to recognize what is allowed and what is not, but he also learns to test how you will react by breaking some rules. At this point, redirecting him to a different activity is the best option. Ignore the behaviors you like to discourage and pay attention to good behavior.

- Stay consistent in your disciplinary strategies like enforcing limits or time-outs (if needed).

- At this stage, tantrums are common because your child is struggling to master his newfound skills and trying to cope up with new situations. Anticipate triggers like being hungry can prevent the incidence of temper tantrums.

- If he has siblings, expect conflicts between them now and then. Teach the toddler not to use aggressive acts like biting or hitting.

C. Preschool Age

- During this stage, kids are still trying why and how things work and the effects of their actions. While learning the appropriate behavior, expect your child to test your limits.

- Understand that there are some forms of frustration that he cannot handle by all himself, guide him to resolve the issue.

- Allow him to make choices by giving positive options within sensible limits.

- Start assigning age-appropriate chores. Provide simple and step-by-step instructions to do each chore properly and reward him with encouraging words.

- Catch him doing good deeds.

- Teach your child to treat others respectfully.

- Help him handle angry feelings positively by talking about it and not by hurting someone or breaking things.

- Use time-outs or removing the reason for conflict in cases of peer or sibling issues.

D. Grade School Age

- Your kid begins to understand the right and wrong, and the advantage of choosing the best option during difficult situations.

- Continue teaching and demonstrating respect, concern, and patience for others.

- Discuss expectations and consequences for not obeying family rules.

- Provide balanced responsibilities and privileges, rewarding more privileges when he follows the rules.

- Refrain from using punishment.

E. Adolescents & Teens

- As your kid grows older, his decision-making skills will be more developed, so balancing your unconditional support and love with clear boundaries, rules, and expectations are a must.

- Show plenty of attention and affection, make time for a daily talk that strengthens the family connection. Avoid long lectures.

- Recognize all your teen's achievements, success, and efforts. Appreciate his good choice of not using alcohol, drugs, or tobacco.

- Talk about respectful and responsible relationships. Know his friends, too.

- Be a role model.

Tips to Enjoy the Journey of Parenting

Have fun. Don't lose your sense of humor. Be happy and joyful while nurturing the child. Laugh at some silly errors your child, or you make along the way. Be your kid's most trusted confidant and best friend. Spend time playing, learning, talking, and passing the legacy to live life with joy, love, and respect.

Accept your child wholeheartedly. Provide unconditional love and support while you enforce kind, firm discipline to keep him in the right direction. Refrain from getting too attached to the comments of other people on your child-whether positive or negative.

Share yourself to your child- your feelings, beliefs, and thoughts. Encourage him to share back. It is an excellent way to fine-tune your kid's brain and inculcates self-regulation skills, acceptable social skills, and open-minded beliefs that enrich his growth and development.

Apply the respect principle. Treat your child in the way you want to be respected. Teach him to be respectful to other people. Respect his boundaries by allowing him to make the first move to approach you or when he prefers to keep quiet. Show respect by acknowledging his feelings and listening to his opinions.

Never discipline your kid in anger. Wait until you are calm to see matters objectively. Use calm words and actions when teaching him the difference between right and wrong behaviors or choices. Avoid yelling or using an angry tone.

Ignore little things. Choose your battles by asking yourself, "Is it important?" This helps you gain self-control and avoid raising your voice.

Give him your full attention. It is a powerful tool to discipline and reinforce your child's good behavior. Spend quality time with him every day to talk about his daily experiences. Encourage him to share his feelings and thoughts.

Be prepared – for troubles and misbehavior. You cannot put your child in a box and order him to do the right things. But, it helps to prepare him for upcoming activities and talk about your expectations. Be prepared for unexpected acts that are caused by external factors, something that you or your child cannot control.

Always be consistent. Always show consistency in words and actions. Match your words with your behavior, or else your child will not take you seriously or ignore what you are teaching him. Most often, children interpret their parents' inconsistency as permission to dismiss their requests and attempts to discipline them. Do not forget that children base their acts and beliefs on what they see from others, especially their parents.

Take time to teach your child. Teaching skills and acceptable behaviors take time to develop. You cannot teach him now and expect that your child will assimilate what you teach in just one sitting. It takes consistent effort and time to instill discipline or develop good behaviors. Establishing a fun, effective daily routine will help you, as well as a behavior plan that includes positive rewards. It is also vital to encourage him to continue practicing the learned skills by being a positive role model, exemplifying what you want him to acquire.

Give positive encouragement. Celebrate your child's success and efforts, no matter how small they are. Giving positive encouragement and praises that are focused on reinforcing his skills or behaviors boosts your child's self-esteem.

Build a positive, respectful relationship with your child. Positive discipline does not destroy your bond or relationship with the child. It allows inclusive disciplinary strategies that let you involve him during the process of setting up the rules and consequences as well as evaluation of his own behavior.

Keep a promise. It may be a deserved reward, a secret, or something that he wants to do, always try your best to give it as soon as possible. It builds trust, and you are teaching him the value of word of honor.

Trust your kid's natural goodness. Basically, all children have an instinct to please you and make you proud and happy. So, trust him and his integrity to make good decisions and choices as he grows up. Create a space for him to do what is right by showing confidence in his skills and abilities.

Have faith in your parenting skills. There is no such thing as a perfect parent, but there is a "good enough" term in parenting. A good enough parent utilizes good enough parenting skills through role modeling. If you are doing your best, giving your time and energy to be a good enough parent, then be confident that you are. Be kinder and gentler to yourself, too.

10 Common Parenting Problems and Practical Solutions You Can Use

1. Temper Tantrums

It is absolutely nerve-breaking when your child has this habit of throwing tantrums in public places. It is important to find the cause- like if he is tired, hungry, over-stimulated, or want something. A child throwing a tantrum will just start crying loud, create absolute chaos, does not calm down or listen, and refrain from conveying the reason.

Possible solutions:

- If you are in a grocery or restaurant, removing him to a quiet area is the best solution or taking him home.

- If at home, sending the child to his room to cool down is a good option. It works for children 5 years and older. After the cooling period, approach your child gently and explain why his behavior is wrong, then encourage him to talk about his feelings or reasons why he misbehaved.

- Be calm and try to handle the situation with lots of patience. Talk to your child and say that he can tell you what troubles him only if he stops his tantrums. It is important to send a message that you are not easily unnerved by his tantrums.

- Have a zero-tolerance policy on temper tantrums and discuss with your child the consequences. Be clear about your expectations.

- Ignore him or continue with what you are doing. Usually, when your child sees that you are affected by his acts, he will stop and tell you what he wants.

2. Siblings fights

No matter how parents try to prevent it from happening, there will always be an incidence of fighting between siblings. Kids have this natural tendency to find a way to irritate each other that may lead to major fights.

Possible solutions:

- Deal with your children, individually after they cool down. Avoid taking sides, be impartial and fair.

- Encourage them to resolve the issue by themselves, in your presence. Do not judge who is wrong or right; let them figure it out. It will teach your children to communicate their feelings and negotiate for compromises and resolutions.

- Set house rules, boundaries, and consequences that include removing privileges.

3. Disobedience

It is one of the issues that parents encounter with their children, which, if not nip in the bud can become a lifelong habit.

Possible solutions:

- Stay calm. Avoid being rude or yell at him. Remember that your child sees you as his first role model and how you deal with the issue will have a great impact on how he will handle his problems.

- Make him understand that you do not tolerate any rude behavior, including disobedience. Explain what is permissible and what is not. Set clear limits and consequences.

- Find the reasons why he disobeys you. Acknowledge his justifications and reasons, but do not validate them and impose the necessary consequence.

4. Aggressiveness

A child who beats up other kids, displays violent reactions, or breaks objects can be extremely stressful. If not resolved early, this can be a life-damaging habits that may cause more serious problems to your child, to you, and other people around him.

Possible solutions:

- Get to the roots of the misbehavior. Find out if the reason for his aggressiveness or angry behavior is triggered by a situation at home or because of an external cause.

- Engage your child in a one-on-one conversation to discuss the misbehavior and find a solution.

- If your child is showing abnormal anger pangs that lead to serious harm, ask the assistance of a counselor or submit him to anger management therapy before it destroys him.

5. Poor Eating habits

With easy access to junk foods and many food options, many children have poor eating habits that deprive them of essential nutrients.

Possible solutions:

- Do not force your kids to eat the foods you prepared. Instead, explain to him the effects of junk food consumption like obesity and health problems.

- Involve him in the preparation of his meals, letting him observe how to prepare healthy dishes. Explain to him the importance of vitamins, minerals, and other nutrients for his growth and development.

- Use healthier ingredients for foods that your kid likes.

6. Modern Device Addiction

Excessive use of modern gadgets and the internet poses constant struggles between parents and children.

Possible solutions:

- Set rules to limit the use of gadgets, television, or computers.

- Supervise what your child is viewing or playing.

- Introduce exciting activities like board games, sports, and other outdoor activities. Challenge him to beat you.

7. Lack of interest to study or do the homework

If your child suddenly shows disinterest in studying his lessons or procrastinate in completing his homework, it is most likely that he is having trouble about the subject or his attention is on other activities like video games.

Possible solutions:

- Try to talk to your child about the possible problem that causes his lack of interest to study. If he needs help, offer to assist him.

- If he is weak in some subjects, inculcate a sense of interest and curiosity by demonstrating how the knowledge applies to real-life situations.

8. Lying

Most children tell white lies, a kind of lie that does cause real harm. Most often, they are not aware that they are lying. They want to avoid circumstances. However, if you allow lying to continue, it may develop to bigger and real lies which include hiding important things or information from you. When lying becomes habitual, it may become an integral part of the kids' character.

Possible solutions:

- Do not punish your child when you catch him lying. Instead, it is necessary to make him realize that it is wrong.

- Encourage him to tell the truth and do not be afraid of you even if he makes a mistake.

- Set boundaries and consequences to discourage him from telling lies.

9. Whining

If your child has the habit of whining or complaining even about inconsequential matters, he is actually seeking your attention.

Possible solutions:

- It is important to listen and talk to him when he whines. Help him find the best solution to the issue by brainstorming together.

- Teach him to communicate his issues or find solutions instead of whining. Assure him that you are always there to discuss what troubles him.

10. Lack of confidence

If your kid shuns any type of social engagement, display aloofness, or does not want to interact with other children, he may be suffering from a lack of self-confidence.

Possible solutions:

- Encourage your child gently to make friends or play with other kids. Avoid forcing him to mix in, let him join in his own volition.

- Make it a point to understand his personality and gradually help him to come out from his shell by boosting his self-esteem.

A Summary of what Parenting Is

Parenting is knowing that your kid is always watching you. Be real and be honest, in words and deeds. Do not hide your shortcomings. Do not be afraid to make mistakes and failures. Avoid blaming yourself too much when you fail to the expectations of others, create your parenting strategies for your child. When you see your him copying your negative habit, call his attention, and work together to correct the problem.

Parenting is accepting that you and your child are two distinct, separate individuals with a different personality. You cannot mold him into your replica and display your traits and talents. His temperament, ways of thinking and feeling, manners, failures, and success will not be the same as yours, no matter how you mold him to be. But you know that he will be an independent, responsible, and disciplined person because you impart all that you want to teach and share.

Parenting is welcoming the thought that you will have a lot of trial and error experience. You cannot do everything correctly the first time, especially if you are a new parent. Even if you have many kids, there are parenting methods that work on your first child but do not produce similar outcomes for your second child.

Parenting is continuously finding excellent ways to guide, observe, listen, speak, talk, and act to become a positive role model for your child. As he grows older, you cannot fix all his problems to ease his journey to adulthood. It is necessary to teach him to problem-solve, choose wisely, and make sound decisions as early as possible, providing autonomy that trains him to face his struggles.

Parenting is different for each parent. It is often dictated or influenced by your upbringing, circumstances, challenges, moods, and the unique personality of your child. Children come to us having a unique set of DNA and inborn qualities that you cannot refuse to acknowledge. It is your responsibility to nurture the dominant traits and talents while helping him accept and correct the flaws and negative qualities.

Parenting is about learning from mistakes- your child and yours. If you fail to handle the situation well during the first time, stop being harsh yourself, and try again. If during the sensitive moment, you make a real mistake or feel out of control, remove yourself from the scene, and have a time out. Once you are cool down, go back and say sorry to your child, then work together to resolve the problem. How you handle yourself gives your child an idea on how to recover from mistakes.

Finally, parenting is a reality. Your imagined concept is far different from what you will experience when you become a parent. Every child presents a different set of challenges as he moves from infancy to adulthood. The challenge of making him eat proper food, disciplining, bonding to fit his personality, educating him on sexual matters, giving the right values, and more will be a constant part of your everyday existence once you begin your parenting journey.

Bear in mind that there are no hard and fast rules or strategies to raise children. There are no absolute answers, too. All you need is a loving heart, an open-minded mind, and continuous effort to become the parent that your child will look up to as a positive role model.

Conclusion

Thank you for reading this book until the end. I hope that it inspires and guides you on your parenting journey.

Remember that parenting is not a marathon or a sprint. It requires time, practice, determination, right skills, and perseverance to get the golden ticket – a respectful, well-mannered child. It is not a competition that you play with other parents. It is building a personal relationship with your child.

Parenting is about providing loving guidance with great purpose- to mold the character and personality of your child. It is about understanding who he is, what he cares about, what are his dreams, what brings him happiness or sadness, and what are his strengths and weaknesses. It is about focusing your time and attention to what matters to him while keeping limitations and boundaries.

Parenting is also learning about yourself as a nurturer, a disciplinarian, a confidant, and many other roles associated with it. If you make mistakes or feel your patience running out, take a time-out, and relax. You become a fine parent when you are happy, calm, and centered. Your health and well-being matters because it helps you become an objective, affectionate, and positive parent.

By being present and aware, your child is also empowering you and teaching you how to become a better person. When you know who you are, you become more capable of helping him understand himself. And when your child knows himself in the deepest sense, he is more confident to manage the challenges that come his way during his journey to adulthood. He can face the world with excitement and a purpose to contribute positively to make the world a better place to live.

Finally, I wish you good luck for being a wonderful parent who believes that you need tools and guides like my book **Positive Discipline: New Approach to Discipline, Positive Parenting, and Everyday Solutions to Parenting Problems** to bring out the best in your child.

Printed in Poland
by Amazon Fulfillment
Poland Sp. z o.o., Wrocław